Dad's own house- keeping book

Dad's own house- keeping book

David Bowers

illustrations by Serge Bloch

technical illustrations by Barbara Smullen

Workman Publishing, New York

Designed by Paul Hanson
Art directed by Beverly McClain

Library of Congress Cataloging-in-Publication Data
Bowers, David, 1962–
Dad's own housekeeping book / by David Bowers.
p. cm.
ISBN-13: 978-0-7611-3667-5 (alk. paper)
ISBN-10: 0-7611-3667-3 (alk. paper)
1. Housekeeping. 2. House cleaning. I. Title.
TX301.B62 2006
648—dc22   2006041760

Workman books are available at special discounts when purchased
in bulk for premiums and sales promotions as well as for fund-
raising or educational use. Special editions or book excerpts can
also be created to specification. For details, contact the Special
Sales Director at the address below.

Workman Publishing Company, Inc.
708 Broadway
New York, NY 10003-9555
www.workman.com

www.dadsownhome.com

Printed in the United States

First printing May 2006
10 9 8 7 6 5 4 3 2 1

Dedication

For my wife, Sharon, and my children, Hugh and Pearse. The house always looks terrific to me when you're in it.

Acknowledgments

I could not have written this book without the considerable help and support I received from my wonderful editor at Workman, Ruth Sullivan. Thank you, Ruth, for your tried-and-tested patience with my frazzled dadditude. Francine LaSala was my guardian angel in getting this material molded into shape and I am endlessly grateful for her concision, precision, and good humor about it all.

Hearty thanks to my agent, Angela Miller, who spurred me along more than she knew by asking, "Aren't you finished with that book *yet*?"

Many thanks and kudos as well to all the dedicated and extremely talented people at Workman Publishing who put so much time and energy into the project.

CONTENTS

CONTENTS

Introduction:

Remember Mr. Mom?

When it came out in 1983, the movie's premise—that Michael Keaton's character stayed home with three children, while his wife, played by Teri Garr, went to (gasp!) an office every day and made big bucks in advertising—was daring, even *groundbreaking*. America marveled at the zany scenes of Dad's (sorry, I mean *Mr.* Mom's) inability to cope with washing machines and grocery stores and diaper changes. Today the joke is all but lost.

These days it's the norm for dads to be involved in the upkeep of the house, at least on a part-time, after-work-hours basis and sometimes even more than that. Recently it's become more common for Dad to be *the* stay-at-home parent. According to the U.S. Census Bureau, "more than 2 million preschoolers in America are primarily cared for by their fathers while their mothers work." And I'm one of those dads.

Welcome to a whole new generation of men doing something our mothers may never have taught us: housework. I raise my two sons and run a busy household while my wife is a cell-phone-totin', travelin', meeting-takin' office drone. I know how to run a washing machine and a dishwasher, make beds and buy clothes, pay bills, shop for groceries. (I might add that I'm an excellent cook.) And I get it all done with a speed and efficiency that leaves me plenty of time to pick up some work on the side and actually play with my kids.

I used to try to "help out" around the house, but like most guys, I saw it as not really *my* job. My wife and I both worked full time outside the home, but while my job was manageable between nine and five, hers would sometimes keep her until eight or nine at

INTRODUCTION

night. Eventually her schedule became so hectic that she rarely had time to be home, let alone do anything around the house, so I began to take on more of the day-to-day duties such as shopping and cooking (although I won't deny that for a long time we kept our local Chinese restaurant on speed dial). However, I still saw what I was doing as "helping out."

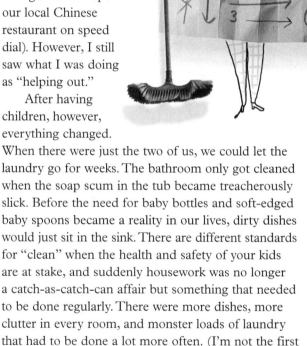

After having children, however, everything changed. When there were just the two of us, we could let the laundry go for weeks. The bathroom only got cleaned when the soap scum in the tub became treacherously slick. Before the need for baby bottles and soft-edged baby spoons became a reality in our lives, dirty dishes would just sit in the sink. There are different standards for "clean" when the health and safety of your kids are at stake, and suddenly housework was no longer a catch-as-catch-can affair but something that needed to be done regularly. There were more dishes, more clutter in every room, and monster loads of laundry that had to be done a lot more often. (I'm not the first parent to wonder how one tiny little person can make such a mountain of dirty clothes.)

With some gentle wifely prodding, I started adding more duties, cleaning the bathroom and doing the laundry, for instance. The more I got into doing stuff around the house, the more it became part of my life. When I got home, instead of flipping on the TV, maybe I'd throw in a load of wash and start making dinner. And you know what? It wasn't so bad. At the end of my wife's first maternity leave, we did a quick evaluation of salaries and decided that she should keep working and I would stay home most of the time and look after the house and kid.

INTRODUCTION

The more involved I got in running the house, the more pride I began taking in what I was doing. Before I knew it, I was interested in doing things right rather than merely seeing them done so my wife wouldn't complain: "Would you mind *not* putting in chlorine bleach when you do a load of darks?" But don't get me wrong. It doesn't mean I woke up one morning and turned into my wife. I may be more on top of things these days, but no matter how many chores I can get through in an afternoon, the fact remains that I'm never going to keep house the way many women would. Neither are you.

Good *Enough* Housekeeping

We're men, and men generally see things differently than women do. Where my wife sees 20 things around the house that need immediate attention, I notice maybe five; where she strives for an "A-plus" level of clean, I'm happy to get by with a "B." Women subscribe to *Good Housekeeping;* men subscribe to a philosophy of "good enough" housekeeping, and that goes double when you're a dad. The key to keeping house Dad's way is to do what's absolutely necessary in the quickest, easiest way possible, and never give a task another thought once it's done. *Dad's Own Housekeeping* shows you how. This is not a book about keeping house as if you were Felix Unger (or to any other standard of "perfection"); it is about keeping one that's comfortable and clean and safe for kids.

The big question for a lot of dads is: How often do I *really* have to do this stuff in order to keep my home in reasonable order? In each chapter, we'll break down the main parts of each job, assign it a priority level, and show you the most efficient way to do it. How can you make your kitchen most functional and then keep it up? Where and how can you keep a clean corner to tend to bills and other household paperwork? And, yes, real men *do* dust and *do* do windows.

Dads do things a certain way, and we think it's a good way. It can take a little adjustment for most women to get used to the new system and go with the flow (see "Managing Expectations," page 3), but most

INTRODUCTION

moms are so grateful to dads who do the laundry and shopping that they wouldn't dream of complaining.

There are definitely other benefits to being a housekeeping Dad. Having the confidence to run my own household while raising and enjoying my kids has been one of the most satisfying things I've ever done. And here's the unexpected bonus: When you're a competent man around the house, able to mind children, do laundry, cook, and clean with equal aplomb, well, chicks really dig it, especially your own wife. Who knew that women could be so turned on by a man who's mopping the bathroom floor or talking about what he's making for dinner?

What Makes Dad's Housekeeping Different

1. We like a no-frills approach.

We generally don't have the time or inclination for extras. We'll clean the bathroom but won't hang those tiny guest towels or freshen up the potpourri. We just want it to function; we're far less interested in imposing our personality on a room.

2. We're doing it for our kids.

Most women have no idea how profoundly today's dads are moved by their children. So much so that we're willing to give up a traditional "manly" image in order to be with our kids, even if that means washing diapers and coaxing crabby little people to nap.

3. We have selective vision.

To stay on top of tasks, it's important for us to establish a routine for cleaning (see page 13). Otherwise, as hard as it is for women to believe, no, we really don't see the overflowing garbage can or the pile of dirty towels we keep stepping over.

4. When we focus, we *really* focus.

If a task interests us, we'll work at it harder than a woman could ever imagine doing. We might let the dishes sit in the sink all day, but we'll remove every particle of melted cheese from the inside of the toaster oven.

INTRODUCTION

How to Use This Book

Dads, choose your cleaning comfort level. This may require some trial and error until you and your partner agree on how often the kitchen floor really needs mopping (see page 2). Then flip through this book to see what applies to you.

Lick-and-a-Promise Clean

Not too bothered about the details? Look for the 5-Minute Attack for each room you're going to clean. These will show you the minimum work required in that room.

Average-Guy Clean

Want everything moderately tidy but don't want to drive yourself nuts? Follow the directions for the Weekly Clean in each room—even if you don't do it every week.

Felix-Unger Clean

Are you a Type-A personality? Each chapter has a Priority Level and a guideline for frequency (daily, weekly, monthly, etc.). Follow these rules and each step to the letter and everything will sparkle.

A Man Around the House:

Getting Psyched Up

M y father never changed a diaper in his life, but he cooked nearly every meal I ate at home. My father-in-law, on the other hand, who rarely set foot in the kitchen unless a meal was already on the table,

GETTING PSYCHED UP

considered the laundry and vacuuming his personal province. In that generation, men helped out when and if they felt like it. It was a bonus if they did chip in and not expected if they didn't. These days things are a little different. It's more common than not that both parents work outside the home, and it's a toss-up who's home early enough to put on the dinner or first in the door to hear that a sports uniform needs to be washed for the next day's game.

Were you a polished hitter the first time you picked up a baseball bat? Not likely. Being in charge of a home takes a little practice, too. In this chapter, we'll get you started on thinking like a housekeeping Dad; after that, we'll move through the tasks in your home and show you how to get maximum results from minimal effort.

Can't We All Just Get Along?

Do you and your wife fight about housework—and do you do it more often now that you have kids? A national survey by the Soap and Detergent Association found that 55 percent of couples with children regularly argue about housework, whereas only one-third of childless couples said it's a point of contention.

One of the reasons for this is that kids, especially when they're preschool age, are exhausting, and small problems, like the dirty socks you left in the family room, can escalate to near-divorce-worthy issues when people are tired. But you can't blame the kids for all the cleaning strife in the family. Even when it was just you and your wife, you did things that might set her off (see page 4).

Women have been in charge of running the house for so long that a lot of them are kind of set in their ways. They think a job isn't finished if it hasn't been done the way they would have done it. Take the kitchen, for example. My wife used to look in the door as I put away the last supper dish and say something like, "I thought you were going to clean the kitchen."

It took a lot of bickering before I finally realized that, in our minds, we were looking at two entirely different rooms. If I had put away the leftover food

and done the dishes, as far as I was concerned, the kitchen was finished for the night. My wife's idea of a "finished" kitchen entailed having every counter gleaming, the floor swept, any obvious spots mopped up (at least wiped with a damp paper towel), the dishtowels hung—neatly. And once that was done, she'd probably undertake some other project, like throwing away those pears I meant to toss last week and washing the fruit bowl.

But she doesn't clean the kitchen most nights. I do. Very quickly, it became clear that we needed to talk out how things were going to be done around here.

Managing Expectations

Just like anything else in your marriage, it all comes down to communicating points of view and negotiating: If your wife doesn't expect the scent of a freshly mopped floor when she sticks her head in the kitchen door after dinner . . . well, then she won't be disappointed.

However, it's not just her expectations that needed to be managed. I was one of those clueless dads who said that *we* weren't going to fill *our* home

GETTING PSYCHED UP

Things We Do—or *Don't Do*—That Drive Our Wives Nuts

So, women do have a few complaints about our domestic habits. I've heard these recurring gripes from a lot of them. So, guys, it doesn't hurt to be aware of how they feel.

- We clear the table nicely, then sweep all the crumbs onto the floor with a casual flick of the hand.

- We do all the dishes and clean the kitchen but somehow always forget to empty the gunk from the sink strainer.

- When we clean the kitchen, we don't wipe the countertops.

- We are apt to leave dirty pans on the stove—with food in them.

- We put leftovers away in the pots we cooked them in.

- We sometimes load dirty dishes into the dishwasher on top of clean dishes.

- We put greasy pans in the sink on top of soaking dishes that will now need to be doubly washed.

- We are much more likely to *load* the dishwasher than to *unload* it and put the clean dishes away.

- We're not big on wiping up the kitchen floor after making a cooking mess—in fact, we don't even see it.

- We toss things in the general direction of the trash can, and if we don't "make a basket," we shrug and leave it where it dropped.

- When we take out the garbage, we don't replace the liner.

- We push aside clearly expired food in the refrigerator or freezer instead of throwing it away.

- We don't notice greasy handprints on cabinets, walls, the refrigerator door, switch plates—or anywhere else.

- When we do the laundry, we rarely look under the bed or the coffee table to pick up balled-up socks or underwear.

- We forget to empty pockets before tossing clothes into the washing machine.

- When we clean the toilet, we seem not to realize that the pedestal is part of the toilet and therefore also needs attention. Who knew?

- We make the bed by pulling the duvet up over crumpled sheets.

GETTING PSYCHED UP

What We Want Women to Know About Our Housekeeping

Men have some comments on the subject for women, too. To keep things running smoothly, it helps to take these thoughts seriously. (But note how much shorter our list is. Women!)

- We don't expect *you* to do things our way. Don't expect us to do things the way you do.

- If you ask us to do something, don't show us how and then check up on us while we do it. Above all, don't hover.

- You're not supposed to be our mothers. Issuing orders or giving instructions . . . well, let's just say it's not very romantic.

- Nor is saying things like, "Oh, I might as well do it myself." (Because we'll let you.)

- If you feel very particular about how the silver should be polished or how your silk undies are washed, we don't mind if you do it yourself. Say so nicely.

- Think of your husband as a business partner. You wouldn't tell an office mate, "You're doing it all wrong! Here, let me rewrite that report."

- We didn't mean to marry a drill sergeant. No white-glove tests after we dust, please,

- Remember, we have different plumbing; there has to be a little give-and-take on toilet seats up or down and some forgiveness for the occasional bad aim.

- If you plan to rewash a dish or refold a shirt, don't ever let us catch you doing it.

- Don't continually set the bar higher. A little appreciation goes further than a running critique.

with every battery-operated, primary-color plastic toy in existence. (So of course my living room is a wonderland of Day-Glo.) I swore that I'd have my kids put their stuff into the toy box every evening so that we could walk on carpet, not a minefield of sharp-edged plastic. Ha! Thank goodness I have tough-skinned feet. "We can't live like this!" I would grumble, flinging stuffed animals into the basket that I put out expressly for that purpose. "What?" my wife would say innocently, looking at the storm-tossed wreckage that used to be our living room. "Oh, the toys. Well, honey, they're just little kids."

GETTING PSYCHED UP

Maybe it helps if you have a big playroom with a door that shuts, but in the long run, that doesn't solve the problem. Talking it out does. Discuss what's expected of domestic partners and kids alike. Make compromises if necessary, but come to clearly stated terms about what is and what isn't acceptable in your household, and who's responsible for what.

It's not as onerous as it sounds, and there are no rules except those you set for yourselves. In the end, I agreed that until our sons were a little older, they didn't need to put away every toy every night. And we had a very simple kitchen discussion. I agreed to add counter wiping to my nightly food-stashing-and-dishwashing routine, but nothing more. I mop the kitchen floor once a week, and we both agreed that if my wife wants it mopped more often, she'll do it herself.

It can work in your house, too. If you promise to put your dirty socks, underwear, shirt, and pants in the hamper every night instead of tossing them on the chair by the door, she might agree to quit leaving her shoes all over the house. If you promise you'll stop harping on the living-room clutter, she can agree to clean the bathroom every other week. And so on.

If you establish up front what will and won't happen, and each of you tries your best to keep your end of the bargain, expecting no more and no less, there won't be as much fighting. Marriage counselors call it communication, but it's good business sense as well: If everybody knows what they're getting, nobody is surprised or unhappy with the results.

What's Really Important Here?

In the simplest terms, the sanity of your household is your most important consideration. Who cares if your bathroom tiles gleam or if you can eat off the floor in the kitchen if no one in your house is happy? Here's the bare minimum that needs to be done daily by all members of your family. Start with these basics and the larger jobs will become that much easier. A hectic morning when everyone's rushing off to school and work is no time to be washing the soaking skillet.

■ Dishes need to be washed every evening.

■ Garbage should be taken out every night.

■ Toys, newspapers, books, CDs, and DVDs should be put away after they're used, or at least every evening.

■ Beds should be made every morning. (Even with a pile of dirty clothes in the middle of the room, when the bed is pulled together and the pillows smoothed, bedrooms seem somewhat clean.)

■ Wet towels, washcloths, and bathmats should be hung to dry properly, not clumped in a heap on the floor, and the shower curtain pulled straight across the tub after each bath or shower. Taking these precautions helps prevent mildew and nasty bathroom stink.

Dad's Own Tool Kit

A workman is only as good as his tools. Here's Dad's arsenal of handy, inexpensive, multipurpose, and generally child-safe cleaning implements and products. With them, you can move through your house like a swift, highly trained one-man SWAT team of pure cleaning muscle.

■ vinegar and baking soda

Housecleaning superheroes. Each fights odors and dissolves greasy dirt. Together, they become a foaming lava run that cleans drains and impresses kids without putting them in danger. What more can you ask from a cleaning product?

■ squeegee

See how scum- and mildew-free this keeps bathroom tiles and glass doors and you'll look forward to a naked squeegee session after every shower.

■ paper towels

Wipe faces, hands, noses, floors, mirrors, and more.

■ rubber gloves

If you think these are not manly, get over it. They'll help you stick your hands in places where you never dreamed so much dirt and gunk could possibly be. If you like having skin on your fingers, buck up and wear the gloves. They come in men's sizes now.

■ wet-dry vac

Dad's secret weapon: This vacuum cleaner can suck up big messes of all sorts, from scattered cereal to spilled milk. No crying here!

GETTING PSYCHED UP

■ **plastic bucket or tub** You just need it, okay? For mopping, soaking dirty stuff, holding supplies—or for soaking your feet after a long day.

■ **all-purpose cleanser** Get a nonscratch version if you have a stone, plastic, or metal sink or tub. Or buy a basic, inexpensive one for sinks, toilets, and extra-dirty countertops.

■ **glass cleaner** This and a paper towel make glass surfaces sparkle so brightly that nobody will notice the dust everywhere else.

■ **stain-erasing sponge** Just dampen the sponge and wipe, and hallway artwork and dirty fingerprints are gone. So cool, kids will color on the walls just to watch you use it.

■ **other small sponges** I prefer a sponge no bigger than 4" × 6" that fits neatly into the palm of my hand as well as into corners and behind faucets.

■ **microfiber cloth** Indestructible, magnetically attracts dust. Buy one for $4 in housewares or 12 for $6 in the car care department.

■ **sponge mop** More controlled than a string mop—and easier to clean. Get one with a powerful wringer. I'm not squeamish, but why slosh around in dirty mop water? Use the wringer.

■ **Swiffer (both wet and dry)** The dry electrostatic cloths quickly whisk away dust and fine debris from any bare floor. Use the wet Swiffer like you would a sponge mop.

Teamwork: After All, This Is a *Family* Matter

No matter who is the primary caregiver in your household, everybody has to pitch in when it comes to running a home. Even if you're a full-time stay-at-home dad, you're not going to be able to manage if your wife or partner isn't doing her share. (Full-time stay-at-home moms have long known this about their husbands or partners.) If both you and your wife work outside the home, your schedules are tight (and, likely, your tempers short), but it's fruitless to point out who worked longer on certain days or weeks and who is therefore entitled to skip or duck which tasks. One way or another, certain amounts of work have to be done.

If Your Kid Is . . .	He Can . . .
2–3	Put toys back in a low toy box, put dirty clothes in the hamper, carry laundry to the laundry area, help feed pets, help wipe up small spills, help make his own bed
4–5	Empty wastebaskets, bring in the mail, help set and clear the table, dust, water houseplants
6–7	Sort laundry, help fold and put away clothes, load the dishwasher, vacuum
8–9	Put away groceries, help make dinner by peeling vegetables and mixing ingredients in a bowl, mop the floor
10–12	Clean his own room, feed and brush pets, walk the dog, change the litter box, mow the lawn, take out the trash
13 and up	Wash windows, wash the car, clean out the refrigerator, prepare a simple meal, do his own laundry, babysit smaller kids

Don't forget about one of your most valuable cleaning resources: your kids. Getting them involved in the daily upkeep not only makes your job easier, it gives them responsibility and helps them feel like part of the team. Plus it prepares them for running their own homes after they leave yours. Getting your kids involved may take a little more time at first (there's a learning curve here, guys, so be patient), but you get the bonus of spending more time with them.

Thirty minutes a day is about the limit for older kids; younger kids have shorter attention spans and probably won't have much success with tasks that take more than a few minutes to complete. Kids of all ages can help you keep house with age-appropriate tasks (see opposite page).

One thing you want to keep in mind no matter how old your kids are: Be as specific as possible concerning what you want them to do. Just saying "Clean up the family room" may not be enough. Instead, give your kids a checklist: Pick up your toys, straighten out the magazines, fluff the pillows.

Finally, you don't have to reward your child every time he or she helps out around the house, but a little positive encouragement goes a long way.

What the Pros Know

When you tackle housework, the main objective is to get tasks done as efficiently (and therefore quickly) as possible. Here are a few tricks the pros use that will speed up your work:

■ **Focus.** Professional house cleaners don't sit down and watch TV or take phone calls. They keep working until the task is finished. It *is* possible (although, granted, it's harder) to do this when you're cleaning your own home. Music will help you focus your attention on the tasks at hand, especially if it's turned up so loud you can't even hear the phone!

■ **Set limits.** Tell yourself: "In two (or three) hours, I will finish the (a) bathroom, (b) bedrooms, (c) kitchen floors, (d) laundry." Watch the clock and make it happen. If you're beating the clock, you're less likely to dawdle over

GETTING PSYCHED UP

polishing the chrome on the taps.

■ **Clear the way.** Enter each room with a large plastic basket and clear things that are in the way of dusting and vacuuming. In the same way that you might pick up before a hired house cleaner comes, you should clear surfaces for yourself before you take out so much as a dust rag. (We'll get into clutter management later on.)

■ **Be adequately armed.** Assemble your weapons and supplies (see Dad's Own Tool Kit on pages 8–9) and make sure they're in good condition and ample supply—whether that means a spare vacuum bag or a fresh roll of paper towels.

■ **Finish first.** While it may be tempting to flit from one task to the next, always finish a task before moving on to another. Don't start cleaning the bathroom and then stop to change the sheets. (The one exception to this rule is laundry; see Dad's Own Laundromat, page 77.)

Create a Routine

My three-year old still asks some nights why he has to have a bath—he's just going to get dirty again, he points out. I don't tell him, but sometimes I feel the same way about cleaning the house. But just as a regular bath removes the grime of another day and soothes a child for bedtime, regular housecleaning helps keep a household calm and functional, and prevents it from tipping over the edge from messiness into downright dysfunction.

So set aside a regular time to do household chores and make it a routine, as predictable as a child's nighttime bath. I find it easiest to do the bulk of my chores in the morning. Every day, once the rest of the family is out the door, I put the baby down to play or cart him along in his Baby Bjorn while I make beds, throw in a load of laundry, swab down the bathroom, or pay bills. Some days I give each room a 5-Minute Attack. Other times I clean one room thoroughly.

Whatever chores I choose, it's always my morning routine, and just like that nightly bath, it keeps my house—and my kids—relatively tidy and clean.

Dad's Plan of Attack

Spotless perfection can't be achieved in a house where kids live, and even if it can, it's not worth it. When your children grow up, they'll remember with fondness that you read to them, helped them with their math homework, and had time to play with them, rather than that the beds were made with hospital corners or the laundry folded with military precision.

For that reason, time management is one of the most important aspects of housekeeping. If you can

> **DAD** *to* **DAD**
>
> **N**eed to start cleaning *now* with no time to read this book? Flip to page 180 for a "30-Minute Pre-In-Law Assault on Dirt" that will leave your house highly presentable.

manage your time effectively, housekeeping will become less drudgery and more of a challenge: Can you beat your floor-washing time from last week? How many

GETTING PSYCHED UP

things can you accomplish before the buzzer on the dryer goes off?

Different systems work for different people. You may prefer to set Saturday morning aside for cleaning the house, top to bottom, or assign an hour a day to each room in the home. (Keep in mind that the kitchen and bathroom will require some daily maintenance, no matter what schedule you devise.) Try out a few systems and stick to the one that works best for you.

Now, Dads, let's get to work.

Dad in Charge:

Kitchen Setup

The way most people run their kitchens is like the story of the woman who always cut the end off a roast before she put it in the pan. When someone asked why, she said she didn't know, but her mother had

KITCHEN SETUP

always done it. When she asked her mother why, she also didn't know, but her mother had always done it. So they called the grandmother, who didn't know what they were talking about. She had sometimes cut the end off because her roasting pan was small and whole roasts usually didn't fit into it.

Your kitchen's set up a certain way—because that may be the way your wife's mother did it or how things got placed when you first moved in—but that doesn't mean it's the best way. If the big standing mixer is monopolizing the counter right beside the stove, making it difficult to set down a hot pan from the oven, or if the stew pot you use at least once a week is tucked away in the back of a cabinet, you're not working in a Dad kitchen—a place where a guy has room to prepare a meal and not take a lot of extra steps.

If you're doing most of the kitchen duty or even sharing it equally with your spouse, there's nothing like reorganization to signal a regime change. So get ready to strip down the countertops and turn your work surfaces into a lean, clean cooking machine. Stock your pantry with foods that make dinner fast and fun, and, along the way, get rid of everything but the most useful pots, pans, utensils, and gadgets.

Dad's Kitchen Overhaul

Restaurant kitchens are tight, cramped spaces where every person is responsible for a certain number of dishes. (They also tend to be brightly lit and quite hot, with lots of people yelling at once. A lot of home kitchens are like that, too.)

Now take a closer look: A restaurant kitchen is organized for maximum efficiency in the tightest possible space: *Cooking space* is sharply delineated from *prep space,* which is very distinct from *cleaning space.* Everyone on the kitchen staff has what he needs right in front of him to finish the job at hand, so he doesn't lose time digging around in cupboards. A good home kitchen, stripped down to the essentials, with everything set up to maximize function, can be like this—only better. Let's rebuild your work space so it operates like a popular restaurant. (Some of us feel like short-order cooks, anyway.)

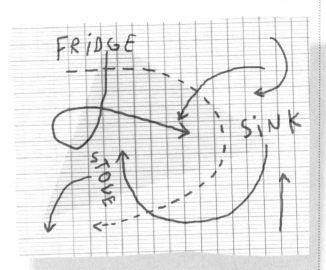

Your Work Triangle

In the kitchen, the "work triangle" marks the tracks between refrigerator, sink, and stove. When you cook, you move from fridge to sink to stove, with pit stops at the surfaces between them. Examine your triangle. Can you move from one station to the other without clipping the kitchen table or another not-so-cleverly-placed object? If you can, great! Skip ahead to "Your Primary Work Space." If you can't, your work triangle isn't, well, working.

What can you change? You're probably not going to move the sink. Or the range, either, with its gas line and built-in ventilation system. But perhaps you can move your refrigerator to the other side of the room—it's your kitchen, after all. (Just don't do it by yourself—and don't ask your wife, who may take a dim view of your plan. Maybe another house-keeping Dad can give you a hand during the day.)

Before you start the heavy lifting, do the math: Measure the room and its furnishings and draw a quick diagram to see if things will fit where you want to put them.

DAD *to* **DAD**

If moving the fridge makes the door open the wrong way, no problem; most modern refrigerator doors can open in either direction. After emptying the door of food, simply whip out your screwdriver and make the change.

Daddy Dough

One of the main obstacles you'll have in reorganizing your kitchen—or, let's face it, doing any household task—is keeping your kids occupied. To keep them entertained while you're working, whip up a batch of Daddy Dough for them to play with. (*Note:* Some play doughs don't require cooking, but this one lasts longer without crumbling and it's more elastic.)

You Will Need

2 cups flour

1 cup salt

2 teaspoons cream of tartar

2 cups water

2 tablespoons vegetable oil

Food coloring

1. Combine dry ingredients in a large saucepan. Over medium heat, slowly stir in water and oil. Keep stirring till mixture is smooth and pulls away from sides of pan into a ball.

2. Dump dough on counter and allow to cool just long enough to handle comfortably. Knead, adding a little flour if necessary, until smooth and elastic, firm but pliable.

3. Divide dough into quarters and color each by kneading in a few drops of food coloring. Store in airtight plastic containers or zipper-lock bags. Discard when dough starts to feel either crumbly or excessively soft.

Your Primary Work Space

Even if your kitchen is tiny, you need one comfortable, clear spot that's your primary work space. You want to be able to reach all the way to the back of the counter, so you have plenty of room to wield a knife, knead bread, or anything you choose. If you don't have such a space, designate one and move all appliances and knickknacks out of it. Ideally, your knives and cutting boards should be within arm's reach.

Clear the Decks!

Cleaning and reorganizing a room as chock-full as the kitchen can be daunting, so let's take it one step at a time, starting with the big and visible stuff.

Clearing off the counters and putting back *only* the items you actually want, use, and need is one of life's simpler pleasures because it gives you stunning instant results. Farewell to the glass jar of dried beans and canister of spaghetti. Adieu to that pile of papers by the phone. And hasta la vista, baby, to that stupid wicker basket of folded cloth napkins that your wife thinks is so charming but has never been used.

> ### DAD *to* DAD
>
> **W**hen in doubt, toss it out. Here's a situation that really works in our favor, even for us cheapskate Dads: If you really miss an old appliance you threw away (which you probably won't), remember that it can always be replaced with a more state-of-the-art—or at least more up-to-date—model.

KITCHEN SETUP

To begin, take everything off the counters, including small appliances such as the blender and coffeemaker, and larger ones, like the microwave and toaster oven, and put them anywhere you can find room that's not a countertop.

Now look at your bare counter and try to imagine yourself chopping, slicing, mixing away in your primary work space without the usual chaotic clutter. What appliances are you using? Does it really make sense that the popcorn popper has been next to the sink all these years?

What you'll begin to see (when you look at it from this vantage point) is that most of the trappings of your kitchen could be stored in a completely different house and you'd never even notice they were missing. I use my food processor constantly, but I use my blender maybe once a year, and it would take up valuable work space on my counter. I love my slow cooker, but the ice-cream machine gets an outing only when my wife wants to use it, which is . . . well, practically never. So why keep it out (or even at all)?

Thinking it through before you start replacing things will give you a clear picture of what should go back on the countertop and where and what should be put away in a cabinet, stored in the garage, given away, or carted to the dump.

It Looks Clean to Me

And that may very well be, but sometimes the Dad perception of clean is not all it could be. So now that you have an idea of where everything should go, you need to scrub those countertops before putting anything back. Sprinkle baking soda on a warm, damp sponge and go to town. For caked-on grease that somehow found its way under the toaster oven and for the water stains underneath the food processor, moisten the spot and sprinkle with baking soda, then go do another task for ten minutes. When you come back, you'll be able to easily wipe away even the most hardened crud. By the way, before you put back any of those appliances, give them a good wipe down, also with baking soda, to remove encrusted food stains or grease.

Putting It Back Together

Once the counters and appliances are clean, put back *only those items that you need and use.* Start with the big stuff: microwave, blender, food processor, cappuccino machine, toaster, toaster oven, and so on—your call. Before replacing them, think about how often you use each item and when. For example, if you haven't used the regular toaster since you got your toaster oven three years ago, get rid of it. When I realized that my cappuccino maker was just taking up space, off to a local charity it went. Don't get overexcited about all the clear space and stack too much stuff back up there. That's your new *work* space, *not* your appliance storage space.

When the big, daily use stuff is back in place, turn to the rest. You may have room in your cabinets to store less frequently used items; more likely, you may have to wait until you've also organized your cabinets and drawers, an in-depth project to save for a rainy day. (If you want to get into the specifics now, turn to Appendix II, page 187.) Meanwhile, pile any extra appliances into boxes to sort later.

Pots and Pans:

Getting Down to Basics

If you've been harboring a nonstick skillet that sticks like crazy or some of those faddish and useless glass cooking pots, you need to look hard at what's standing between you and the pans you need to get dinner made. You might have a beaten-up old wok that's your favorite item, so keep that. But otherwise, clear out the excess, the rusted, the unused, and the warped. You need only the following basic pots and pans in your kitchen:

DAD *to* **DAD**

Always use wood or plastic utensils in your nonstick pans to keep them nonstick. When the coating starts to wear off, replace the pan. A scratched nonstick surface is worse than a regular "sticking" surface and sheds unhealthy particles of the coating into your food.

KITCHEN SETUP

Cooking

- lidded saucepans in at least three sizes: 4 quart, 2 quart, 1 quart

- large nonstick sauté (vertical-sided) or omelet (slant-sided) pan

- large nonstick skillet with lid (perhaps

seasoned cast iron, for frying or roasting)

- large pot or Dutch oven for making pasta, boiling potatoes, steaming vegetables

- steamer basket

Roasting and Baking

- roasting pan and rack
- 12-cup muffin tin
- two 9" × 5" loaf pans
- two 11" × 17" baking sheets

- stoneware or glass casserole and baking dishes, one deep (for lasagna), one shallow (for gratins or casseroles)

Season That Pan

Cast-iron pans can't be beat for sautéing or frying. The seasoning process smoothes the iron's rough surface and makes it as nonstick as any high-tech pan. To season a new pan, or to reseason a pan that you have scrubbed free of rust or dirt (steel wool works best), wash it in warm water with a little dish soap. Set the oven to 350°F while heating the empty pan over low heat on the stovetop. As soon as it's dry, wet a paper towel with one or two tablespoons vegetable oil and rub all over both inside and out. Put the pan in the oven upside down with a cookie sheet on the rack below it to catch any drips and bake for an hour. Never wash a cast-iron pan with soap. To clean, scrub with hot water and a plastic scouring pad, then wipe dry with a paper towel.

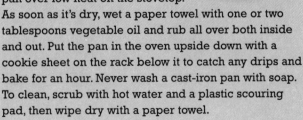

KITCHEN SETUP

Paper Trail

Sometimes the paper associated with your kitchen can rival even that of your home office—and few things make a room look messier than having piles of paper everywhere. How can you get it under control?

■ Keep takeout menus in a manila file and tuck into a drawer designated for this purpose, or slide the folder, upright, between drinking glasses (or cereal boxes) and the cabinet wall or onto your cookbook bookshelf.

■ Stash appliance user manuals and warranties the same way. Staple purchase receipts to the front of the manuals. (Remember to discard the manuals if you discard the appliance.)

■ Clip coupons immediately. Neatly store them in an envelope that you can tuck away in a drawer or tack up on a bulletin board. Make it a once-a-month task to toss the expired coupons.

■ Store cookbooks on a shelf that's not right next to your work space. Nothing gunks up a cookbook faster than stove splatters or food-covered hands.

■ Buy a Plexibook holder: It holds thick cookbooks open, keeps splatter off, and can stand on a counter or, with its strong magnetic backing, can stick to the fridge.

■ If you like to download recipes from the Internet or clip them from newspapers, invest in a cheap binder and a three-hole punch to store them. If you hate the recipe once you've tried it, tear it out and toss it.

Knives

What's in Your Arsenal?

Knives are fun to work with, and it's great to have a knife for every slicing, chopping, and cutting task . . . but do you really need so many? Here are the essentials every self-respecting cook needs:

■ large chef's knife (can double as carving knife)

■ 6" utility knife

■ 3" to 4" paring knife

■ serrated bread (and tomato) knife

■ knife sharpener (see page 29)

KITCHEN SETUP

Keeping knives loose in a drawer dulls and nicks the edges, and sliding them in and out of those fancy wooden blocks wears away their sharp edges. Store knives on a magnetic knife rack screwed into the wall near your work space, which keeps them easily accessible but out of the reach of your children.

Quick Tips for Maintaining the Order

Once everything's been set right, the main problem we have is keeping it straightened. It's one thing to reorganize things and store them away; it's quite another to put things back night after night where you've assigned them. Here are some ways to make sure you don't undo all your hard work in the first week you use your new, more functional kitchen:

1. Post a user guide. Until your family gets used to the new setup, stick up a couple of notes such as "Napkins here" or "Salad spinner, rice steamer, Cuisinart, here."

2. Put organizers in place. If you want something to stay somewhere, give it a place to be. Drawer and space dividers for cabinets are readily available in housewares stores, and they make it a lot easier to reserve designated spaces.

3. Stay diligent. Fight for your clear work space by discarding packets of condiments or giveaway cups, and if you do use that cappuccino maker for a dinner party, put it away again.

4. Don't be disheartened. If stuff starts to stack back up on your counter, don't give up and decide your kitchen is meant to be cluttered. Just clear it off again.

5. If it feels really wrong, change it. Can't get used to having your spatula in the drawer to the right of the stove? Move it back where it came from.

Dad Does Dinner:

Fast Food

After a day of work, most adults probably would prefer to put their feet up and ponder what to order in. But when you have kids, dinner-time rolls around bright and early, and kids who don't eat in a timely manner are *cranky*. There's no getting around the fact that part of overall housekeeping is the feeding of the people who live in the house.

COOKING

When it's Dad's turn to cook—which it will be now and then, whether he stays home with the children or works a full-time job outside the home—he wants to make the whole thing quick and efficient, not to mention tasty. This chapter will show you how to do that, with tricks for shopping and keeping the pantry stocked, along with advice on quick prep and even a few one-pot dishes that everyone in the family will be happy to eat. (You can also check out *Dad's Own Cookbook* for lots more recipes to ease the task.)

Stocked Up and Ready to Cook

It's great if you have time to amble from market to market, selecting the freshest and most succulent fruits and vegetables, newly baked breads and meat cut to order—but that doesn't resemble the life of any parent I know. What busy Dads need when it's their turn to cook dinner is a well-stocked pantry that will let them pull together a tasty, kid- and parent-friendly meal in less than 30 minutes.

Make a copy of this checklist and take it to the supermarket—you'll have storable food that will last for weeks (don't forget to freeze the meat if you're not using it in a day or two).

Breads
- ☐ bagels
- ☐ sliced bread
- ☐ English muffins
- ☐ hot dog/burger buns
- ☐ pita, tortillas
- ☐ _____

Dairy
- ☐ butter
- ☐ cheeses (hard, soft, shredded)
- ☐ cottage cheese
- ☐ cream cheese
- ☐ eggs (store in refrigerator only)
- ☐ half-and-half
- ☐ milk
- ☐ sour cream
- ☐ yogurt
- ☐ _____

Meats and Fish
- ☐ chicken breasts and/or nuggets
- ☐ deli meats
- ☐ hamburger (in 1- or 1½-lb. packs)
- ☐ steak and/or pork chops (one chop for each family member)
- ☐ Italian sausage links (sweet are more family-friendly)

COOKING

- ☐ fish filets or fingers
- ☐

Frozen
- ☐ berries
- ☐ concentrated juice
- ☐ ice cream
- ☐ pancakes/waffles
- ☐ Popsicles
- ☐ vegetables
- ☐

Canned Goods
- ☐ beans
- ☐ soups
- ☐ stock/broth
- ☐ tomatoes (whole, crushed, puréed)
- ☐ tomato paste
- ☐ tuna
- ☐ vegetables
- ☐

Jarred and Dry Goods
- ☐ cold cereal
- ☐ crackers
- ☐ hot cereal
- ☐ ketchup
- ☐ mayonnaise
- ☐ mustard
- ☐ nuts
- ☐ olives
- ☐ pancake/waffle mix
- ☐ pasta/noodles
- ☐ peanut butter
- ☐ popcorn
- ☐ raisins
- ☐ rice
- ☐ pasta sauce
- ☐ salsa
- ☐

Beverage
- ☐ coffee
- ☐ cocoa
- ☐ juices
- ☐ powdered drink mixes
- ☐ seltzer
- ☐ tea (black, herbal)
- ☐

Misc. Cooking
- ☐ dried herbs and spices
- ☐ hot sauce
- ☐ oil
- ☐ soy sauce
- ☐ stock or bouillon cubes
- ☐ vinegar
- ☐ Worcestershire sauce
- ☐

Misc. Baking
- ☐ baking powder
- ☐ baking soda
- ☐ brownie mix
- ☐ cake frosting
- ☐ cake mix
- ☐ cornmeal
- ☐ cornstarch
- ☐ flour
- ☐ honey
- ☐ molasses
- ☐ sugar
- ☐ vanilla extract
- ☐

Fresh, Not Very Perishable
- ☐ apples/oranges
- ☐ carrots/celery
- ☐ garlic
- ☐ onions
- ☐ potatoes
- ☐

COOKING

Short-Order Dad

BC (before child), my wife and I used to wander in from work, have a drink, watch TV, and either cook or order in around 9:00 P.M. With children, there is no downtime when it's dinnertime; dinner has to be on the table by 6:30, 7:00 at the latest.

When your kitchen is organized and efficient, it becomes easier, despite after-school activities and late nights at the office, to schedule mealtimes and actually sit down for meals together as a family, an "old regime" tradition that I learned growing up and enjoy keeping. (I'm not so picky about elbows on the table and napkins in the lap, though.)

Though at one time I swore that my offspring wouldn't spend one unsupervised minute watching TV, now I see the TV as heaven-sent for dads making

A Cutting Edge

A dull knife can be dangerous because it requires you to use more force, so if it slips, you're going to get cut badly. Keeping knives sharp makes them easier and more efficient to use. As tempting as they may be, avoid electric knife sharpeners, as these may actually grind away the edge of your knife. Instead, purchase a quality *steel* (those long metal cylinders with handles, available wherever kitchen knives are sold) and give each knife a few swipes at a 20° angle before each use. A steel magnetically realigns the ions on the edge of a knife's blade and also removes the microscopic metal burrs that produce dull blades. Every two years or so take knives to a professional sharpener.

dinner. I plonk my sons down in front of some child-friendly show with a healthy predinner snack like carrot sticks or cucumber slices with hummus, sliced apple, or cut-up orange wedges. Then I cook as quickly and efficiently as I can (thanks to having everything handily arranged), and soon after Mom comes home and gets settled in, we're ready to sit down at the table together.

Express Prep

Do I plan in advance? Sort of. Early in the day I say to myself, like a flight attendant, "Chicken or pasta? Beef or fish?" Then it's a matter of what needs to be defrosted, what has to be chopped before cooking, and how long I can put off what I have to get done.

Meats can be defrosted the night before in the refrigerator (if you're really on top of things), in a bowl of room-temperature water during the day, or in the microwave at the last minute. It's a good idea to get meat thawed early so you can marinate, then slice it into strips, cubes, or whatever's called for. Vegetables can be washed and chopped when—okay, *if*—you have a little downtime, and set aside in the refrigerator in plastic storage tubs until you're ready to use them. It is now also possible to find fresh prepped vegetables at the supermarket. Just empty the package straight into the pot and you're good to go.

COOKING

Following are some quick-prep tips for the nights Dad does dinner:

■ Hate peeling potatoes? Serve rice or noodles more frequently—or keep the skins on, which is healthier anyway. Just be sure you give the skins a good scrub first.

■ Use strong, clean kitchen scissors instead of a knife to snip herbs directly into salads and sauces, and to cut cold chicken breasts, hardboiled eggs, pizza, fresh mushrooms, or pita.

■ Use your hands whenever possible— to tear up lettuce and toss a salad, crumble firm cheese into a sauce or onto a casserole.

■ Chop anything you can in the food processor, from vegetables to herbs to bread for bread crumbs. Use the grating attachment to shred carrots, onions, etc., to shorten cooking time. Note: Carrots in 1" chunks can take 30 minutes to cook, but ⅛"-thick rounds will be ready in 10 minutes.

■ Take advantage of the salad bar at your grocery store. It costs a little more, but sometimes it's worth it. Cooked chicken and ham can be chopped (if it isn't already) and tossed into an omelet or dropped into a quick cream sauce and served over rice. Marinate chopped fruits and cleaned berries in a little orange juice. When you finish dinner, spoon on a little fresh cream or plain yogurt for a yummy, healthy dessert.

■ Use thin pastas, such as angel hair, for quick cooking—3–4 minutes.

■ Couscous cooks a lot faster than rice— just pour boiling water over it, cover, let sit for a few minutes, and it's done.

■ To peel soft fruits like peaches, tomatoes, or nectarines, drop them in boiling water for less than a minute. Remove with a slotted spoon and run under cold water. The skins will split and you can pull them right off with your fingers.

■ When making stew, chili, or pot pie, buy meat already cut into cubes.

■ Store olive oil and other frequently used ingredients, like pepper and salt, right by the stove so you won't have to open the cabinet every time you need them.

■ To quickly prep garlic, lay the cloves on a cutting board, cut off the base end, smack them with the flat side of a knife blade, and remove the skin. Sprinkle salt over the cloves, make a few preliminary chops, then drag the flat of the knife blade over the salted cloves. The abrasive action of the salt will help the knife pulverize the garlic.

■ Use thin cutlets and fillets of meat for fast, even cooking. Pound thick chicken breasts with your fist or a meat mallet (much more fun) for a few seconds to even them out before cooking.

■ Rinse and spin dry 3 or 4 days' worth of various lettuces for salad. Wrap each day's serving in a paper towel–lined, zipper-lock plastic bag and store in the fridge vegetable drawer to keep them fresh and crisp.

■ Make salad dressing (see page 38) for the week instead of each night.

My Rice Cooker and Me

I always thought a rice cooker was one of those one-use gadgets, but after I had a toddler who would often eat nothing but rice, I changed my mind. Mine cost less than $20 and holds six cups of cooked rice, more than enough for a family of four. You can put the rice on in the morning and come home up to twelve—yes, *twelve*—hours later and the rice is still hot and fresh and perfectly cooked. Even brown rice, which takes twice as long to cook and ends up scorched when I make it on the stove.

What's more, if the rice is ready, dinner seems ready. I only need to stir-fry some meat and/or vegetables, or ladle on some spaghetti sauce for my toddler, and all that hungry crankiness evaporates. What more could a guy ask of an appliance?

COOKING

Dad's menu

Quick Kid Dinners for Dads on the Go

The secret to keeping yourself and your family happy at mealtime is to make things that are fun to eat, nutritious, and also easy to prepare. These recipes satisfy all those needs in our home.

But you don't need to stop at these six. Keep the pot boiling by thinking about how to put together a meal with ease. It doesn't have to be meat, potatoes, and vegetable. Kids get bored with that. Consider foods such as sautéed chicken breasts with soba noodles and green peas, or a vegetable

stir-fry over quick-cooking rice noodles.
Peeling potatoes takes a long time when you
could just slice polenta off a store-bought
roll or use your rice cooker (see page 31).
Use frozen vegetables (tastier than canned)
to cut down on prep time and buy meat in
presliced pieces (such as pork medallions
or chicken tenderloins). Use extra shots of
flavor such as soy sauce and sesame oil or
herb seasonings. Make dinner easy on
yourself and you'll enjoy it more, both the
cooking and the eating.

Dad's Fajitas

Most kids love Tex-Mex food, and why wouldn't
they? It tastes good and they can eat it with their
hands! Many supermarkets sell sliced beef for fajitas,
or you can use ground beef instead and make tacos.
Just brown the meat and add ½ to 1 teaspoon of
cumin to it. With green salad (or chopped lettuce and
tomatoes to top your taco), dinner is served. If you
have store-bought salsa, grated cheese, and sour
cream, you can plonk the components on the table
and let everyone assemble their own.

SERVES 4

You will need

1½ **pounds round steak or boneless,
skinless chicken breast**

1 **green pepper**

1 **onion**

2 **tablespoons vegetable oil**

1 **lime or lemon**

8 **corn or flour tortillas**

About 1 cup grated Cheddar cheese

Salsa

Sour cream (optional)

COOKING

1. Slice the beef or chicken, pepper, and onion into thin strips. Heat the oil in a skillet over medium-high heat. Add meat and brown for 3–5 minutes. Add pepper and onion, and sauté for 6–8 minutes, until meat is well browned and cooked through and vegetables have started to soften.

2. While the meat is cooking, wrap the tortillas in a clean kitchen towel. Lay them on a plate and heat in the microwave on high for 45 seconds. Place all the ingredients on the table.

3. Squeeze the lime or lemon juice over the meat, season with salt and pepper, and place in a bowl, and serve immediately, letting everyone add garnishes to taste.

Dad's Roast Chicken

With this extremely Dad-friendly, hands-off technique, you can have a beautiful roasted chicken on the table in under an hour, no basting or fussing. Don't be shy about turning up the heat or it won't work right. A cast-iron skillet really speeds things up here; if you don't have one, use a roasting pan, skip the stovetop heating, and add about 15 minutes to the roasting time.

SERVES 4

You will need

One 3- to 3 1/2-pound whole chicken

3 tablespoons olive oil

Salt and pepper

Preheat the oven to 475°F.

1. Heat a dry, empty 10-inch cast-iron skillet over medium-high heat for five minutes. (A larger skillet, such as 12 or 15 inches, is fine, but don't use a smaller one.)

2. Rinse the chicken under cool running water and blot dry with a paper towel. Drizzle with the olive oil and sprinkle generously with salt and pepper. Use your hands to rub the oil, salt, and pepper all over the outside skin and inside the cavity.

3. Wash your hands, then carefully place the chicken in the hot skillet, breast side up. It will sizzle. Use a potholder to slide the skillet into the preheated oven.

4. Roast for 45 minutes or until a thermometer in the thickest part of the thigh registers 165°F. Test for doneness by sticking a fork in the thigh; it's done if the juices run clear.

Cook a package of egg noodles, toss with butter and Parmesan, and prepare a frozen vegetable such as green beans as sides. Depending on the size of the chicken—and your family—leftovers can be enjoyed for days in sandwiches, salads, or chicken tacos.

Dad's Quick-Baked Potatoes

You can "bake" potatoes really quickly in the microwave, although you won't get the crisp skin and creamy interior that distinguish a real oven-baked spud—but who's got an hour to wait for baked potatoes! Try this technique and have it both ways.

SERVES 4

You will need

4 large baking potatoes
   (Idaho russets with thick skins are best)
Olive oil
Salt

Preheat the oven to 425°F.

1. Scrub the potatoes well under cold running water and pierce each several times with a fork.

2. Microwave the potatoes on high for 5 minutes. Turn them over and microwave another 5 minutes.

3. Remove the potatoes and rub them with a little olive oil and salt on their exteriors. (Careful—they'll be hot!)

4. Transfer directly to the oven rack and roast for 10 minutes. Wearing an oven mitt, squeeze each one gently to be sure it's soft throughout. These can rest for 20 minutes or be served right away (ideally with butter and sour cream).

COOKING

Dad's Own Fish Sticks

Kids don't care if fish is good for them—the fact is, not many of them like it, including my own kids. That's why I devised these easy-to-make fish cakes. Shaped into savory fingers and quickly fried in minimal oil and served with ketchup, they're the best way I know to sneak some Omega-3 fatty acids into my picky eaters. I serve these with green peas and store-bought frozen French fries.

SERVES 4

You will need

1 small onion

3 slices bread

One 15-ounce can salmon
   (or 1³/₄ cups cooked fish fillets)

1 large egg

¹/₂ teaspoon salt

¹/₄ teaspoon black pepper

Cooking oil

¹/₂ cup bread crumbs (crushed corn flakes or
   cracker crumbs work very well, too)

Ketchup, lemon juice, and/or tartar sauce,
   to serve

1. Peel the onion, then chop fairly small in the food processor. Add the bread and pulse until it forms coarse crumbs.

2. Drain the salmon. Add the salmon or fish, egg, salt, and pepper to the crumbs in the food processor and pulse until just combined. (Don't overprocess it into a paste.)

3. Place the bread crumbs on a plate. Shape the salmon mixture into 12 sticks, about 1 inch

wide by 3 inches long.

4. In a skillet, heat about ½ inch of cooking oil over medium-high heat. (It's hot enough when a drop of water sizzles in the pan.)

5. Roll the fish sticks lightly in the bread crumbs and fry in the oil for about 5 minutes per side, or until golden brown.

6. Serve with ketchup for the kids and tartar sauce or lemon juice for the adults.

Sausage and Spinach with Pasta

Maybe other people's children gobble up spinach with gusto, but my oldest will only eat it when it's served with pasta, cheese, and sausage. Those telltale green shreds don't exactly disappear, but they become less offensive.

SERVES 4

You will need

1 pound round pasta, such as small shells, or macaroni or rotini

1 pound Italian sausage, sweet or spicy

One 10-ounce package frozen spinach

2 tablespoons all-purpose flour

2 cups milk

1 teaspoon salt (optional)

1/2 teaspoon black pepper (optional)

1/4 teaspoon chile flakes (optional)

2 tablespoons butter

Grated Parmesan cheese for the table

1. Bring a potful of salted water to a boil over high heat.

2. Meanwhile, cook the sausage in a skillet over medium heat. If it's in casings, simply squeeze it out into the pan and discard the casing. Cook the sausage thoroughly, breaking it up, and drain off the fat.

3. When the water comes to a rolling boil (makes big bubbles), drop in the pasta and swish it around once. When the water returns to a boil, reduce the heat to medium and simmer till done (most packages say how long to cook it—often about 6–8 minutes). Stir once or twice to prevent clumping.

4. When the pasta is almost done, put the spinach into a bowl and microwave it, following the directions on the package.

5. Sprinkle the flour over the warm sausage and stir well. Cook for an additional minute or two over medium-low heat, then slowly stir in the milk, stirring well to prevent lumps from forming.

6. Add salt and pepper if using, and chile flakes if using, and simmer gently, stirring frequently, until sauce is thickened.

7. Add drained spinach and drained pasta to the skillet and toss well to combine. Serve immediately with Parmesan cheese.

Dad's Own Salad Dressing

This is a classic vinaigrette that's great on any sort of greens and can also make a quick marinade for chicken or beef.

MAKES 1 CUP

You will need

$3/4$ **cup extra-virgin olive oil**

$1/4$ **cup wine vinegar**

1 tablespoon Dijon mustard

1 clove garlic, minced

$1/4$ **teaspoon sugar**

$1/4$ **teaspoon black pepper**

Salt to taste

1. Combine all ingredients in a glass jar with a tight-fitting lid. Shake hard to emulsify. Taste and adjust seasoning if needed.

2. Store in the refrigerator for up to a week. Shake well each time you use it.

Cooking Shortcuts

Even if you like to cook, it doesn't mean you want to spend your whole night doing it. To speed up getting your meals on the table:

■ *Preheat the oven.* The finished food will be much tastier if it doesn't have to warm along with the oven.

■ *Turn up the heat.* Cook on high! Seared meat tastes better, not just because the juices get "sealed in" but because it brings the natural sugars to the surface, where they caramelize and turn a tasty, crusty brown.

■ *Nuke it!* Try cooking bacon, fish, and vegetables in the microwave, but avoid preparing other meat and baked goods this way—usually the time saved isn't worth the flavor lost.

Keep it Warm

"Honey, I'm gonna be late . . ." You get the call when the meal's ready to be put on the table. How can you keep food warm without ruining it?

■ Set the oven to 140°F and place your meal inside, in either the cooking pots or a serving dish. Cover with foil to prevent getting the food crusty or too dried out.

■ Mashed potatoes will stay hot in a covered pan for nearly an hour if you mash them swiftly (without milk), clap a lid on top, and wrap the whole pot in a dishtowel. Set it on the stove, away from the burners. When ready to serve, stir in microwave-heated milk.

■ Toss pasta with a tablespoon of olive oil, or noodles with a pat of butter, to prevent them from becoming gummy. If needed, nuke briefly just before serving.

■ Plunge cooked vegetables into cold water; drain when they're cool. Keeping them warm in the oven or on the stove will turn even the firmest carrot to mush. When you're really ready to sit down, reheat them in the microwave.

COOKING

Not Again! Dad Does Leftovers and Food Storage

When I was a bachelor, and even after I was first married, I'd rather eat my arm than leftover food. I didn't mind raw ingredients in my fridge, but I resented seeing tubs full of old meals. It's a guy thing. We hate seeing the same stuff trotted out day after day on the dinner table. (This rule doesn't hold up for meat, such as turkey and roast chicken. They're not leftovers: They're sandwiches.)

Once you have kids, though, you get more frugal about throwing food away. And little kids love repetition. If they liked it the first time, they *love* it the second. So half a dish of macaroni-beef casserole stops looking like bin-fodder and starts looking like lunch.

I do have some rules on leftovers and food storage, though:

■ *If the serving dish is at least half full, store in the serving dish.* If you have half a casserole or a plate of sliced meatloaf left, don't transfer it to a range of plastic containers. Cover it with foil or plastic wrap and store it in its dish.

■ *Make an airtight seal.* Whether you're using the same dish or using takeout food containers, seal the food up tightly so your fridge doesn't smell like your dinner.

■ *If it's less than a serving, throw it away.* Don't fill your fridge with tiny dabs of leftover food. You'll just have to throw them away later.

■ *Toss out dressed salad.* People always try to save salad. It doesn't work, people. Throw it away. It will be a wilted, yucky mess in the morning. Save yourself the heartache.

■ *Is it soup yet?* You don't have to drive yourself nuts re-creating leftovers for a new meal. Either serve them as they were (reheated in the microwave), make sandwiches when possible, or utterly disguise them as soup. Mashed potatoes, for example, make a good thickener for any vegetable soup—and any leftover vegetable can go into a new stew or be the base for a soup.

DAD'S OWN HOUSEKEEPING BOOK   *41*

COOKING

If You Run Out, Punt

Level-headed Dads don't freak out if they're missing some basic ingredients for a recipe—they use these clever substitutions:

If You're Out of ...	Substitute ...
buttermilk	plain yogurt
sour cream	plain yogurt OR mix 1 cup milk + 2 tbs. white vinegar or lemon juice (for cooking only)
sweet cream	$1/2$ cup milk + $1/4$ cup melted butter (only for adding to a dish, not for desserts or whipping)
self-rising flour	1 cup all-purpose flour + $1 1/2$ tsp. baking powder + $1/8$ tsp. salt
baking powder	1 part baking soda to 2 parts cream of tartar
$1/2$ cup sugar	$3/4$ cup light corn syrup
light corn syrup	honey
powdered sugar	granulated sugar finely ground in blender or food processor
unsweetened chocolate	3 tbs. cocoa + 1 tbs. cooking oil
semisweet chocolate	3 tbs. cocoa + 1 tbs. cooking oil + 3 tbs. sugar
sherry or vermouth	apple juice with wine vinegar or lemon juice added (for cooking only)
tomato paste	ketchup or chopped and sieved canned tomatoes
Worcestershire sauce	splash of A1 steak sauce
Dijon mustard	yellow mustard + a pinch of sugar + a splash of white wine vinegar
dry bread crumbs	crushed cornflakes or crackers
brown sugar	1 cup white sugar + 2 tbs. molasses

COOKING

■ *Use it or lose it.* Four days is the limit. If you haven't eaten it by then, you're not going to.

■ *When in doubt, throw it out.* Did everyone hate your turnip gratin or broccoli mousse? Let it go, Dad. Don't trot it out again, thinking they won't remember. They will.

Smart Shortcuts [for Dads Who Love to Cook—and Hate to Clean]

We Dads enjoy cleaning up after cooking about as much as watching Lifetime movie marathons. But cleaning up is part of the job. Here are some ways to make it a little easier as you go:

■ *Put ingredients away as soon as you finish using them.* Take one egg from the fridge, not the whole carton. Measure rice into the pan and put the package back into the cupboard. It speeds cleanup later and, more important, keeps the counter clear for work.

■ *Clean as you go.* If you spill flour all over the counter, wipe it away when it happens, not at the end of the meal prep.

■ *Rinse food-processor parts after chopping fresh vegetables.* Give the bowl, lid, and blade a rinse under the hot tap and set them in the drainer.

■ *Reuse pots whenever possible.* If you've sautéed chicken breasts in your nonstick skillet, set them on the serving (or dining) plates and quickly wilt fresh spinach leaves in the same pan with a splash of water. Lift egg noodles out of the cooking water with a large slotted spoon and use the boiling water to quickly cook fresh

DAD *to* DAD

Use low-fat spray oils for greasing pans and baking sheets instead of spreading butter or fat. You can even buy special pressurized spray bottles and fill them with olive or other healthy cooking oil, such as canola.

broccoli or green beans. (*Never* reuse a pan or dish that held raw or partially cooked meat without washing it first in soap and hot water.)

■ *Keep your dish drainer cleared* so you can give things that don't get "dirty" a quick rinse and forget about them. After I drain pasta in my colander, I put the pasta back in the pot, give the colander a quick rinse and wipe in hot water, and set it in the drainer. The same goes for the salad spinner—a plain rinse is all it needs. When it's time to wash the dinner dishes, these big items are dry and ready to be put away.

■ *Keep a few inches of hot, soapy water in the sink.* When you're through using something, drop it in to soak. If the crud doesn't dry on, you'll have a lot less scrubbing to do.

■ *Never get your roasting pans dirty.* Cover the bottoms with heavy-duty aluminum foil, making sure you have enough foil to fold over the edges. This foil is strong enough not to tear when you spoon up the juices to baste. (If you use the pan drippings to make gravy

or sauces, carefully scrape them off the foil and add them to your simmering stock or whatever base you're using. When cleaning up, lift out the foil and discard. The pan should be completely clean, but if anything does slip through, it should require only a wash instead of scraping and scrubbing.

■ *The same goes for baking sheets.* Grease or spray the foil to keep foods from sticking. When the empty pan

COOKING

has cooled, recycle or discard the foil—your baking sheet should be ready to go back in the cabinet without touching water.

■ *Always line cake pans with waxed paper* and grease (or spray) the paper once it's in place. You'll still have to wash the pan, but you won't have to *scrub* it.

■ *Bake muffins or cupcakes in paper baking cups.* Don't overfill the cups—two-thirds full should be fine. If you're careful and don't drip any batter onto the pan (or wipe off drips with a damp paper towel), you won't have to wash the muffin tin at all.

■ *Paper towels are fast and clean.* Use them for draining fried foods, for wiping counters and stovetops and hands, for wiping a greasy patch on the floor in front of the stove. To cut down on waste, reuse paper towels whenever possible and remember that they can be composted.

■ *Do away with serving bowls and platters.* Dish out directly from the stove, or if your kids are old enough, let them get their own, buffet style. For just-family meals or dinners with close friends, put the cookware on trivets or potholders on the table and let people serve themselves.

Dad Cleans Up His Act:

Kitchen Patrol

You've organized the kitchen to make it work for you, you've cooked a fast dinner that everyone enjoyed and thanked

PRIORITY LEVEL:
High

NEEDS ATTENTION:
Daily

you for making while they helped clear the table (ha!), and now it's cleanup time.

KITCHEN PATROL

The 30-Minute Nightly Cleanup

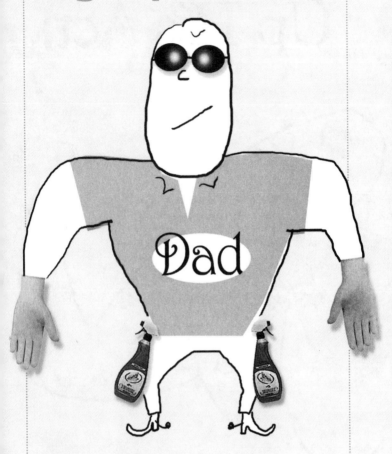

O ther rooms in the house can be made presentable with a 5-minute dash, but the kitchen is always going to take a little more time because there are a number of tasks that must be done daily. Use this streamlined approach to finish them all, and you might find yourself coming in under the 30-minute deadline. Whatever you do, work to keep your time under half an hour (unless you're cleaning after a party or a big cooking session); that way, you won't have to dread the kitchen cleanup.

You Will Need:

SPONGE

RUBBER GLOVES

DISHWASHING LIQUID OR DETERGENT

BROOM, SWIFFER, OR VAC

SPONGE MOP

PAPER TOWELS

Put Away the Food

2 MINUTES

■ Throw it in plastic lidded containers and toss it in the fridge. Don't eat it, just put it away.

Wash the Dishes

14 MINUTES

■ Even if you're handwashing, you can do it in this amount of time using the technique on page 53.

■ If you're loading the dishwasher (see page 50–51), don't spend a lot of time pre-rinsing. Let the machine do its job.

Wipe Everything Down

5 MINUTES

■ Wipe down all the countertops, including washing any cutting boards.

■ Take a swipe over the interior of the microwave with a damp sponge to prevent spatters from drying on.

■ Wipe the top of the stove and under the rings, if necessary, to remove cooking splashes.

■ Give the fridge door handle and cabinet door handles a quick going over with a damp sponge.

■ Drain any dishwater and rinse out the sink.

KITCHEN PATROL

Do the Floor
4 MINUTES

■ Sweep with a broom, or use the Swiffer or a handheld vacuum to remove all crumbs and spills.

■ If the spill is wet or there's dried food on the floor, spot-clean with a paper towel or break out the sponge mop.

Finishing Details
4 MINUTES

■ Remove all crud from the trap in the sink drain and discard it.

■ Rinse your sponge and toss it in the microwave for 1 minute (see opposite page).

■ Take out the trash.

Set Up the Coffee
1 MINUTE (SPECIAL DAD BONUS)

■ You've come this far, the kitchen is spotless, now go the extra mile and set up the coffeemaker for the morning. Pour in the water and measure out the coffee. My wife *adores* it when I do this. You wouldn't believe how many brownie points I get. It's worth it.

DAD *to* DAD

Mineral buildups on the coffeemaker can mar the flavor of the best beans. Clean the coffeemaker every two months by running 2 cups white vinegar and 2 cups water through it. Cool vinegar and run it through again, then discard vinegar and follow with two carafes of plain water to rinse. Coffee will taste fresher and smoother.

Ideally, before your favorite TV show starts. Can Dad do it? Yes, he can! Use this chapter to race through tasks, whether you're handwashing with my speed-technique or loading the dishwasher aerodynamically using your spatial-relations skills.

Dishwasher Dynamics

There's one word we men really respond to when it comes to getting dishes clean: *dishwasher.* Without it, an annoying task is a burden. Of course, not everything you use *can* go in the dishwasher (so try to use only dishwasher-safe implements when you cook), and yes, some cooks still don't have dishwashers. Poor guys! Whichever way you wash them, just remember that the dishes are not officially done until they are put away.

■ Let the dishwasher do what it was made to do. Most modern machines require no pre-rinsing, and many have a pot-and-pan scrubber setting.

■ If all the food is cooked except one item, dish onto plates (keeping them warm in the oven if necessary) and put the empty cooking pots in the dishwasher. Loading them now will only take about 60 seconds and will make the whole job seem faster and more manageable after dinner. If you've created a full load, run the dishwasher while you eat so it will be ready to unload and refill when you're ready to deal with the dinner dishes.

■ Never put fine china, silver, or crystal in the dishwasher unless your machine has a

DAD *to* **DAD**

How do you keep your kitchen sponge clean and sanitary? Nuke it! Dampen the sponge with warm water, put it in the microwave, and "cook" for one minute on high. If you don't do this every couple of days, your sponge will spawn bacteria and smell really funky. *Be careful:* A really powerful microwave can set the sponge on fire, so keep an eye on it.

Loading the Dishwasher the Aerodynamic Way

While most of us guys take great pride in loading the trunks of our cars to balance the load and fully maximize the limited space, we somehow forget everything we know about spatial relations when it comes to loading the dishwasher. Here's the way to do it—that will put even your wife's dishwasher-packing skills to shame:

■ The water comes from the center of the machine, so the objective is to face all dirty dishes, cups, etc., toward the center.

■ Plates go on the bottom, one to a slot, never on the diagonal, and facing the center.

■ Large items go near the outside; load smaller items in size order as you make your way to the center.

■ Frying pans and other flat pans can be loaded on the outside or sometimes on top of the glasses.

■ Stack drinking glasses and mugs with the open side down, toward the water jets, and as close together as possible on the top rack. This is your everyday stuff; it's not as fragile as fine crystal and china. If wineglasses won't stand upright, try them at a 45° angle. Improvise with combinations to ensure you fill every possible millimeter of space.

■ Load knives and forks with handles up. If the sharp end is up in the basket, you risk stabbing yourself every time you reach for something else from the dishwasher.

■ Load spoons or cooking utensils, like spatulas, with the used side up. They have wider surfaces to clean than forks and knives, and this will ensure they get more splashing action.

KITCHEN PATROL

A white film on glassware means hard water. Use a commercial rinse to prevent.

Tip bowls forward to maximize water contact.

Check the filter basket (on bottom, above drain) and empty often.

Casseroles and baking dishes go on their side so they don't block the spinning arm.

Don't bother pre-rinsing plates for modern washers.

KITCHEN PATROL

Clean and Green

Baking soda is my favorite kitchen cleaner, as it appeals both to the environmentalist in me and, even better, to my inner cheapskate. True, there are hundreds of spray cleaners and scrubbing cleansers, but chances are none of them work as well as a plain box of baking soda for greasy kitchen dirt. While ordinary cleaners may only slide over baked-on grease, baking soda bonds with the particles and dissolves them into a soaplike residue that you can quickly wipe off of any surface without scratching or marring. Sprinkle it on liberally and scrub with a wet sponge, then wipe thoroughly. You can also use it on pots and pans and even to clean a not-*too*-blackened oven.

delicate cycle specifically for these items—and always put them in the dishwasher by themselves, not with the everyday dishware.

■ When the drying cycle ends, unload the machine (and put everything away) so it will be ready for stray dirty dishes as needed.

Help for the Handwashers

■ Wear your rubber gloves with pride. With them, you can plunge your hands into really hot water. And you can root around in all sorts of muck and not care how gross it is.

■ If you have a single sink, use a plastic basin for washing and the sink for rinsing. If you have a double, use one side for washing and the other for rinsing.

■ Run sponges or dishcloths swiftly over the surfaces while washing. Make short work of scrubbing with a scrub sponge or a no-nonsense plastic scrubber (remember not to use metal on nonstick surfaces).

■ If you run out of space in the dish drainer, spread a clean dishtowel on the clean countertop and stack clean dishes on it (on a slant for air to get underneath so they dry).

■ Don't dry dishes—that's what dish drainers are for. After you wash, let them dry in the drainer. If the rinse water is hot, most will dry without getting water spots. If it's part of the house rules that whoever washes also puts away, try to do it before turning in for the night.

No Dishwasher? The 20-Minute Dinner Party Cleanup

This simple technique of dishwashing lets you clean your kitchen fast, using only one pan of dishwater and finishing in record time. Don't stop to dry anything or refill the water. Use a clean towel on the counter if you run out of space in the dish drainer. This way, you can handwash the dishes for a dinner party for four while the guests are chatting and the after-dinner drinks are being poured.

1. Clear a space on the counter to spread out a clean, dry dish towel. Fill your dish basin with hot soapy water. Start washing while the water is still running.

2. Wash glassware first, when the water is cleanest, and stand it upside down on the towel.

3. Follow with all the plates, bowls, china, and any glass, pottery, or stoneware dishes and stack them neatly in the dish drainer.

4. Wash all utensils next and stack them in the utensil holder on your drainer. (Extras and big serving pieces can dry on the dish towel with the glassware.)

5. The upright plates make a base to support pots and pans, which you wash next in the slightly murkier water. Finish off with any big miscellaneous items such as woks or colanders and balance them on top.

6. Leave everything to drip dry. Wipe the counters and walk away.

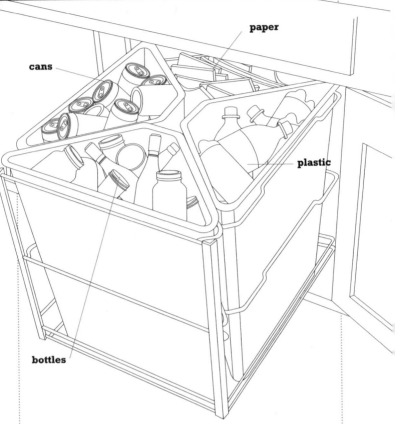

cans

paper

plastic

bottles

Talking Trash

It's not that much fun, but somebody has to do it. Just like with any other kitchen task, doing a little at a time makes the job easier, so make taking out the trash part of your daily routine. Better yet, if your kids are old enough, why not make it part of theirs? Here are some other trash tips:

■ Sort your garbage from your recyclables right in your kitchen by having separate disposals for regular garbage, paper, aluminum cans, bottles and other glass, and plastics.

■ An in-sink disposal is a great way to get rid of eggshells, vegetable peelings, and leftover bits of dinner. In certain cities, however, regulations prohibit their use, and in some older houses the plumbing might not be up to the job. If you don't have a disposal, don't peel into the sink or you'll only make more work for yourself. Instead equip your kitchen sink with a strainer tub, which is perfect for peeling into.

■ Try not to peel vegetables directly into the garbage bin. While this may seem like the most direct way, many is the time that peels fly all over the place, sticking to walls behind the bin, landing on the floor, or even behind cabinets where you'll never reach them. Instead, peel into a basin, tub, or bucket, or even a mixing bowl on your counter. Dump all your prep garbage in your trash bin at once when you're done.

■ If you have a garden, collect organic waste to use as compost. Keep a plastic basin handy for coffee grounds, eggshells, toast scraps, potato and carrot peels, onion skins, and so on. In addition to saving work, you'll also be doing the environment a big favor: Separating organic waste from inorganic can reduce your trash by about 40 percent! Never put meats or fats into your compost, as these are an invitation to vermin.

The Weekly Kitchen Clean

In a perfect world, you'd tackle all smudges and splatters when they happen; in the real world, pick a day of the week to concentrate on getting the kitchen really clean and go to town on them then. When you're in the throes of whipping together a meal, it's easy to forget to wipe your hands before you open a cabinet—and just as easy not to notice you made a mess or forget to wipe it off if you did notice. Evaluate your counters, cabinets, light switches, and drawers and pinpoint the problem areas. Grab your trusted old friends, baking soda and a warm, damp sponge, and wipe down all these surfaces—and don't forget about the small appliances. (We'll get to the big ones later.)

You Will Need

■ **all-purpose spray cleaner**

■ **powdered cleanser or a nonabrasive liquid cleanser**

■ **lemon juice, baking soda, or vinegar (if you want to stay away from the heavy chemicals)**

■ **ammonia**

■ **sponge**

KITCHEN PATROL

- a couple of clean, absorbent towels (not the good ones)
- glass cleaner
- paper towels
- broom and dustpan
- vacuum cleaner
- basin
- sponge mop, wet Swiffer
- wet-dry vac

At Clean Range

It's not enough to know how to use the range; you also have to know how to clean it. The stovetop and the oven are susceptible to really heinous messes because anything that drips or splatters on them gets baked on. You could take the Easy-Off route in tackling these messes, but here are some other suggestions:

- Always wipe up spills as soon as you can, before they get cooked or baked on. Believe me, it will save you lots of time and elbow grease later!

- If you don't want to use toxic oven cleaners, put a shallow glass pan (not metal!) of ammonia in the oven and let it sit overnight. The next morning, remove the pan and air out the oven for 15 to 20 minutes. Scrub with a sponge, hot water, and plastic scrubber.

- If ammonia sounds too messy or smelly, mix a pint of warm water with ½ cup white vinegar and a squirt of dishwashing liquid, then liberally sponge it on the inside of your oven. Let it sit for 15 minutes, then scrub with a plastic scrubber or scrubbing pad.

- If you can't remove the last bits of black, baked-on carbon, rub very gently with superfine sandpaper. If you do it carefully, you can remove the stain without scratching the enamel surface.

- Run grimy burner shields and the grates from gas ranges through the dishwasher every other week to remove cooked-on food.

DAD *to* DAD

Don't scrub burnt-on food. Fill the pot with water above the burn line, add 3 tablespoons baking soda, and boil.

Sweat the Small Stuff

Even if you don't use them that often, you have to clean them. I'm talking about those small appliances that get gunked up from use or caked with dust from disuse. Here are five things to remember when cleaning:

1. Don't let spills dry. It's much easier to wipe cake batter off a stand mixer or milk off a cappuccino foamer before it dries to something insidiously shellaclike.

2. Avoid extra washing. If all you did in the food processor was make bread crumbs, wipe it with a paper towel and put away. (This only works with nongreasy, nonsticky foods.)

3. Be green. Cleansers and chemical cleaning sprays can easily seep into crevices of small appliances—and into your food. Instead, use a damp cloth sprinkled with vinegar or baking soda to clean exterior surfaces.

4. Get a cover. I thought the quilted, flowered toaster cover my wife got as a gift was silly until I let the toaster sit uncovered for a few months.

5. Use the dishwasher. Most appliance accessories, like food-processor bowls and mixer attachments, can be washed on the top rack.

Washing the Dishwasher

Loading and unloading the dishwasher can be big tasks, but the fun doesn't stop there. Not only is your dishwasher a machine that cleans, it's a machine that needs to be cleaned—inside and out. Here are some essential tips:

■ If your dishwasher has a removable filter, empty and rinse it periodically, as well as checking to be sure the spray nozzles on the spinning arm aren't clogged.

■ If you've got hard water, you'll see it on the frosty buildup on your drinking glasses and the lime scale in the bottom of the dishwasher. Buy a container of ascorbic acid (or citric acid powder) at the drugstore. Put a few spoonsful into the detergent holder and run the dishwasher, empty, through a hot cycle.

KITCHEN PATROL

■ If you can't find ascorbic acid, fill a cup with white vinegar or with baking soda (not both!) and put it in the top rack. Run a hot cycle with no dishes.

■ In a pinch, put a couple tablespoons of unsweetened lemonade mix in the detergent holder. There's enough ascorbic acid in the mix to clean out your lime scale.

■ Keep the exterior clean with a few shots of glass cleaner and a paper towel, or wipe with a damp sponge sprinkled with baking soda. Rinse the sponge clean and wipe again. Dry with a paper towel.

Raiding the Fridge—and Not the Fun Way

The refrigerator can easily become the dirtiest thing in your kitchen if left on its own. Outside, grease and grime accumulate on the top and doors, and the handles collect crud like crazy. Inside, food goes bad, sauces spill, meat juices run; if it wasn't so cold in there, it would be a bacteria factory! Every week you should:

■ Evaluate expired food and toss it instead of just pushing it aside. (Actually, you should do this every time you look in the refrigerator, but unless it's furry, oozing, reeking, or even moving on its own, bad food is not something we men notice.)

■ Wipe the inside with baking soda and a damp sponge. You don't have to go nuts taking everything out; simply move the food away from the walls and wipe around what's in there.

■ For the outside, work from the top down. Clear off the top,

What's That Smell?

Is there a mysterious odor emanating from your sink? Something may be trapped in there. Dump in 1/4 cup baking soda, give it a quick scrub with a sponge, then pour more down the drain and add white vinegar. It will fizz wildly (as chemistry buffs and parents of fourth graders know); rinse it down with hot water from the tap. The fizzing soda will freshen and deodorize.

sprinkle baking soda, and wipe well with a warm, damp sponge.

■ Sprinkle baking soda on the sponge and moisten it with a small amount of warm water. Wipe down the front and sides, leaving the dirty handle for last.

KITCHEN PATROL

Every three months or so, give the fridge an overhaul, starting from the inside and working your way out:

■ Take out all the food—dead or alive. (Put things that aren't in airtight containers, like that package of chicken, in a tub or fridge bin where they can sweat, drip, bleed as much as they want.)

■ Give the inside shelves a quick, dry wipe, removing crumbs and other loose detritus.

■ Take your trusty box of baking soda and liberally sprinkle all problem areas— and there will be many. Add a small amount of water and let the soda work its magic while you go on to another task. If the bins or egg or ice trays are really grotty, wash them in the sink with warm, soapy water or in the dishwasher if they fit.

■ Inspect the things you took out. Note expiration dates, foul odors, inappropriate greenness, and any kind of fuzz. Throw out anything that's going bad or is already gone.

■ Head back to the refrigerator with warm, damp sponge in hand. Wipe the surfaces clean, including the shelves.

■ When the bins, etc., are dry, replace them and return all the food to the refrigerator. If you're ambitious, organize it in a useful order.

■ Leaving an open box of baking soda in the fridge really does keep odors down. Rip the top off a small box and set it at the back, where it will absorb strong food smells. Replace it with a fresh boxful every three months.

Floor It!

A lot of people make a big deal of floor cleaning, but it's really not so bad—especially when you have a wet-dry vac revved up and ready to roll. I swear by mine.

■ A little spot-cleaning goes a long way. If oil splatters onto the floor while you're cooking, wipe it up immediately with a paper towel rather than tracking it around the kitchen. Same goes for dropping dry food: Keep a sturdy small brush and dustpan or a cordless vac in easy reach in the kitchen and *use* them.

■ Before washing the floor, clear things out that are easy to move. Your garbage bin could stand in the hallway for the time it takes to sweep or vacuum your floor; your kitchen chairs can be stacked seat to tabletop the way they do in restaurants at closing time. (Save the big moving for Spring Cleaning; see page 163.)

■ Don't skip the dry sweep or vacuuming.

It's tempting to try to save some time and go straight to the mopping, but it only makes more work. When your wet sponge mop gets caked up with crumbs and dirt, instead of cleaning the floor, you wind up just relocating the debris to other areas. (Most vacuum cleaners have a setting for bare floors. Use it.)

■ Fill a basin with warm water and floor cleaner or sprinkle in some baking soda if you prefer. Start at the point farthest from the door

The Wet-Dry Vac: Dad's Best Friend

My wet-dry shop vac used to live in my woodshop. Then I had children and a lot of wet stuff appeared on my floors. Juice. Cereal. Spit-up—and worse. Now I store the vac in the kitchen and bring it out whenever there's a spill.

Wet-dry vacs are essentially the bare bones of a vacuum cleaner—a hose and a barrel. Many models both blow and suck. A filter seated in the center of the barrel catches small particles when you're using it as a dry vac, or the hose can be used like a leaf blower to blow away dust (or inflate an air mattress, with an adapter). They're very handy for quickly sucking up dirty water after wet-mopping the floor. They come in all sizes, many small enough to keep in your kitchen pantry, but the bigger ones have much more sucking power.

KITCHEN PATROL

and scrub the floor clean with your sponge mop. Squeeze out your mop every five back-and-forths—or more frequently for a really dirty floor. Mop your way right out of the kitchen. You can let the floor air dry or lay down a clean absorbent towel and use it to skate across the floor to dry it.

■ Alternatively, break out the wet-dry vac. With the dry vac, you can vacuum up all stray crumbs, dust, and dirt. Then, with the wet vac, you can splash water around the floor, scrub any stains with a sponge mop if necessary, and suck up the wet stuff.

The Super Bowl:

Scrubbing the Bathroom

When it was just my wife and me, the bathroom was a relatively low-maintenance spot that we cleaned every couple of weeks or so. It was a place where we could take long relaxing showers or

PRIORITY LEVEL:
High

NEEDS ATTENTION:
At least once a week

BATHROOM:

5 Minute Attack

You Will Need:

CLEANSER
TOILET BRUSH
SPONGE
GLASS CLEANER
PAPER TOWELS

Gather the Towels

1 MINUTE

■ Pick up all dirty towels and stray dirty clothes and toss them into clothes hamper.

■ Hang clean towels, including a guest towel.

Tidy the Tub

1 MINUTE

■ Put stray bottles back in shower caddy or line them neatly along inside wall.

■ Straighten bathmat.

■ Pull curtain evenly along length of tub. Close shower curtain or doors, ignoring soap scum until weekly cleaning.

Clean the Toilet Bowl

1 MINUTE

■ Lift lid and seat. Sprinkle in some cleanser and scrub bowl vigorously at waterline.

■ Tip brush up to swipe all the way around under rim.

■ Use sponge to clean toilet seat and dust that collects around edges.

■ Flush toilet and rinse brush in the clean water as bowl refills. Shake water out of brush and return it to holder.

Finish Up with the Sink

2 MINUTES

■ Put away stuff that collects here— hairbrushes, blow dryers, razors, beauty products. (See Making It Fit, page 67.)

■ Sprinkle small amount of cleanser (a light dusting is faster to rinse) onto damp sponge and wipe basin and back edge. Rinse.

■ Lightly spritz faucet, fixtures, and over-sink mirror with glass cleaner and wipe dry with paper towel.

Dad's Own Spray 'n' Leave

This trick is a great example of Dad multitasking and saving some elbow grease at the same time. Instead of spraying and scrubbing, spray tile cleanser—or vinegar, which is just as powerful and much "greener"— on your bathroom tile and leave it to do its work. Go do something else. When you come back, all you'll need to do is a quick wipe with a wet sponge rather than a scrub.

BATHROOM

soaks or get caught up on magazine reading. Now not only do the kids develop a hundred reasons to need Daddy *right this minute* every time I slip into the bathroom, but the room requires a thorough cleaning at least once a week—and sometimes more often.

A Family Affair

The good news about bathroom maintenance is that you don't have to do it all by yourself. With a little patience, you can train your family to help you keep it up. Here's a list of easy things most family members can do:

■ Cap shampoo bottles and leave them upright.

■ Wipe down shower doors and walls with a squeegee after every shower; shake or wipe water off shower curtains.

■ Remove hair from the catcher before it gets trapped in the drain.

■ Drape bathmat over the side of the tub to dry.

■ Hang wet towels open and straight on the towel bars so they can dry properly.

■ Toss dirty towels in the hamper.

■ Return soap to the soap dish, not melting in a pool of water on the edge of the sink or tub.

■ Cap toothpaste and wipe up any glops.

Earth-Friendly Drain Cleaners

When a drain backs up, most of us rush for strong chemical solutions, but there are far gentler options. If a plunger or plumber's snake doesn't work, try one of these:

■ For drains that are merely sluggish, pour 1 cup baking soda down the drain followed by 1 cup white vinegar. Allow to fizz for a few minutes, then pour in a kettle of boiling water. Repeat until the water drains freely.

■ If the drain is actually clogged, bring out the big gun: washing soda. Washing soda is sodium carbonate, a highly caustic version of baking soda. (Do *not* use washing soda if a commercial drain cleaner has been used on the same clog.) Pour 1 cup washing soda into the drain and leave it to soak through. Once the water drains, follow up with the baking soda and vinegar trick above.

■ Rinse sink after brushing teeth, shaving (that means you, Dad), or washing hands.

■ Replace the toilet paper after the last sheet is used (the appropriate direction for the paper to roll is your call).

When bathroom users keep up with these little tasks daily, the once-a-week cleaning is no biggie.

Making It Fit

With shaving equipment, hairbrushes, hairsprays and gels, makeup, and medication, cabinets in the bathroom overflow more often than toilets. Also, nothing accumulates dust and gunk faster than items left out in a moisture-filled space, so keep as many items tucked away as possible. If you don't have enough storage space to fit everything, it's time to downsize and make room.

BATHROOM

Be a Squeegee Man

A squeegee easily removes excess water from shower doors and tiles. Tile grout is especially susceptible to mildew and fungus, which love wetness. Eliminating moisture eliminates unwelcome spores. And don't forget those hard-water stains that, given enough time to set in, won't ever leave, and soap scum, which has a tendency to dry in impenetrable layers. With a quick rinse and squeegeeing after every shower, you can wipe out scum and stains before they become a problem. Oxo makes a good squeegee..

What's great about a squeegee is that it's like a toy, and kids—especially younger ones—think it's fun to use. If you can convince family members to embrace the squeegee lifestyle, you'll pretty much never have to scrub shower walls again (well, you can try).

■ Inspect the contents of your medicine cabinet and throw away expired products.

■ Toss stuff you don't use. If your wife hasn't styled her hair with her curling iron since 1988, she's probably not going to be looking for it anytime soon. (But ask her about it first; she may know something about the return of the "Curly Girl" hairstyle.)

■ Keep only the open bottle of each product you use in the bathroom; store spares in the linen closet or elsewhere in the house.

■ Reading materials have a tendency to collect hair and lint, not to mention the damage moisture does to the pages. If you want them nearby, try a chest of drawers or a magazine rack just outside the bathroom door.

■ If your wife usually does her nails in the bedroom or the family room, don't store the equipment here. Ask her to tuck those little bottles of nail polish, nail files, and whatnot in the room where she uses them, in a basket or whatever ingenious storage device you or she can think up.

■ Keep only a limited number of towels in the bathroom—one spare for each family member should do the trick—and store the rest on a linen-closet or bedroom shelf.

The Weekly Bathroom Clean

Five-minute touch-ups are fine when guests are coming over on short notice, but you need to *really* clean your bathroom once a week to keep it hygienic. It will take you no more than 30 minutes each week, and it will keep this high-traffic area significantly cleaner—at least, much cleaner than I was used to in my pre-Dad days. That's important whether you have little kids toddling around and fondling the toilet bowl or big kids contributing to the mess with more hair products than you ever thought possible.

Also, staying on top of the bathroom cleanup prevents much bigger problems later, like soap scum that's so set-in you'd consider replacing the bathroom tiles or a toilet pedestal that makes you think twice about sitting down.

To make cleaning the entire room and all its parts easy and efficient, start from the top and work your way down. That way, all dirt moves downward—any remnants to be vanquished when you wash the floor.

Toilet Paper Storage Solutions

Toilet paper is one thing you definitely want to have on hand in the bathroom. Under the sink is a common place to tuck the tissue, but if you're already past capacity there or don't have under-the-sink storage, here are some alternatives:

- Invest in an over-the-toilet storage rack and keep spare rolls on the bottom shelf, within easy reach.

- Check out storage-specific catalogs for more portable options, which range from double holders to ones that hook onto the toilet tank and hang on the side of it to very handy plastic or stainless steel cylinders that sit in the corner behind the tank and hold as many as six rolls of toilet paper.

- Here's a chance to transform something like a gift basket from pretty and pointless to practical as you create smart storage (and make your wife happy at the same time). Stuff basket with rolls of toilet paper and keep it beside the toilet.

BATHROOM

Also leave the sink and countertops for last since you'll be using them when cleaning everything else.

You will need

- all-purpose spray cleaner

- powdered cleanser or a nonabrasive liquid cleanser

- lemon juice, baking soda, vinegar (if you want to stay away from the heavy chemicals)

- nonabrasive scrub sponge

- squeegee

- clean, absorbent "work" towels (reserve some old ones for cleaning)

- large plastic container

- toilet brush

- glass cleaner

- paper towels

- chrome polish or stainless-steel cleaner, if desired

- basin or bucket

- sponge mop, Swiffer, wet-dry vac (or all three)

All Clear!

Before you take a sponge or mop to anything, get bathroom clutter out of the way. Once you've put everything away that belongs behind cabinet doors

Scum, You're Outta Here

Soap scum is a waxy buildup of soap residue, dirt, and skin cells that's resistant to wiping—and to soap. It requires an acid to break it down; there are lots of products with ammonia and borax, but straight vinegar works just as well. This is a good time to don your rubber gloves—unless you *want* to reek of cleansing acids at tonight's poker game.

Dampen shower walls (and doors if you have them) with hot water and pour white vinegar onto a warm, damp sponge. Wipe down the walls (and doors), using as much vinegar as necessary. If a section still looks suspiciously scummy, dry it with a towel or squeegee to see if scum is gone; if it isn't, go over it again. Or you can use a spray bottle filled with white vinegar, then squeegee the tile. Rub down especially stubborn areas with a heavy-duty scrub sponge with lots of scouring power.

and in drawers, clear out everything else that isn't built in: the tissue box (and holder), toothbrushes and cup, soap dish, shower caddy, toilet brush, guest soaps, candles, etc. Although it might seem like a hassle to remove everything from the back of the toilet or out of the shower before cleaning, clearing the decks actually speeds up the job. Why waste time shifting things to clean around and under them?

The Bathtub and Shower

The shower walls are the highest point in the bathroom you clean regularly, so they're your first target.

I used to avoid scrubbing the shower and tub because it seemed like too much trouble. But with young children, nightly baths are standard and you don't want to put your precious morsel, no matter how filthy she is, into a filthy tub. The trick to no-hassle scrubbing is to get in and get out as quickly as possible. Here's how:

1. If you have one of those removable (controllable) shower-heads, dampen shower walls by directing the head at them. If you don't have one, fill a large plastic cup (one of those 20-ounce freebies you got with fast-food lunches) with warm water and splash down the walls. Spray the damp walls with the tile cleaner of your choice and leave it to do its work. Sprinkle powdered cleanser into the wet tub and give it a good rubdown but don't rinse.

2. With a sponge, or the sponge side of your squeegee (if it has one), work the tile cleaner into the shower walls, scrubbing any stubborn spots with the edge.

3. Turn the water back on. Spray or slosh the walls and tub clear of cleaners, rinsing from top to bottom. If you keep your elbow higher than the shower nozzle, the water won't drip down your arm.

4. Pull the squeegee's rubber edge down the shower walls to remove water. If you don't have a squeegee, wipe the walls dry with a clean towel.

BATHROOM

It's Curtains for You

Shower-curtain liners and plastic or fabric all-in-one shower curtains are just as susceptible to mildew and soap scum as shower walls are. But guess what— most plastic shower curtains and liners are machine washable. Set the washer for a warm wash and add one cup of baking soda. For plastic curtains and liners, add two or three hand towels to help rub them clean. When the rinse cycle begins, pour in one cup of white vinegar. You can add the vinegar at the start of the wash if waiting is a hassle, but adding it last will ensure that your curtain is spotlessly clean.

The Toilet

Keeping the toilet clean is the most effective way to keep the bathroom smelling good. It's also a fast, relatively uncomplicated task. All it takes is a toilet brush, a little cleanser, and a few paper towels (more hygienic than using a sponge).

DAD to DAD

Wax your shower? Hey, it protects your car from water damage! After cleaning, apply liquid car wax to shower tiles and grout, buffing it off with a cloth as you would your car. (Just don't get it on the floor or tub, as it will create a dangerously slippery surface.) The wax will keep squeegeed shower walls gleaming for months, and you'll smile a little smugly as you watch the water bead every time you take a shower.

Speaking Dad to Dad, don't be seduced by fancy toilet-cleaning products. Electric toilet brushes with spinning heads and special cleaners that "cling" under the rim promise miracles, but they don't work better than a basic can of cleanser and a round-headed brush with stiff bristles. Spend your money instead on replacing your toilet brush regularly, as soon as the bristles flatten—probably every six months.

Maybe you've heard that dumping a can of soda into the toilet bowl will remove stains, but so will basic cleanser or half a cup of bleach left to soak. And look at the price difference: A buck

for a single-use can of soda or a buck for a can of cleanser that will clean a toilet fifty times? Your call. **(WARNING: Never mix cleanser and bleach. The combination releases dangerous hydrochloric gas!)**

1. With the lid and seat up, shake cleanser into the bowl and scrub briskly. Scrub especially hard at the waterline and under the rim. Leave the sudsy cleanser to work on the crud and to bleach stains. You can flush as you're leaving.

2. Wipe down the rim, seat, and lid. Note that just cleaning the top sides isn't enough. The undersides show when

Blue Water Blues

I used to be a fan of those blue tank tablets and the way the blue water helped keep rings and mold stains from forming quickly and kept odors down. But after some Web research, I found out they're not all they're cracked up to be. They contain thickening agents that affect the siphoning action of most toilets, preventing them from flushing properly. Plus, the bleach concentration in the tablet can damage the rubber flapper, causing your toilet to "run" constantly. You're better off just keeping your bowl clean. Besides, cats and dogs don't like to drink blue water.

BATHROOM

Fight Odors the Manly Way

Like most guys, I don't think a bathroom *should* smell "flower fresh" or "like a spring breeze." It's a bathroom, not a meadow. Instead of using bathroom deodorizers, I rip off the top of a box of baking soda, place it behind the toilet, and change it every three months. It's cheap, environmentally friendly, and low tech—and it actually absorbs odors rather than masking them.

the lid is up, revealing many bad things! And don't forget the area behind the lid, including the bolts.

3. Wipe down the tank and handle, as well as the exterior of the bowl and the base itself. The pedestal can get particularly nasty. Not only do dust, hair, toilet paper lint, and grime build up here, but we—and especially our sons—don't always hit the target.

4. Flush the toilet and rinse the brush in the clean water as the bowl refills. Then shake the water out of the brush into the toilet before you put it back in its holder.

Sink, Mirrors, and Countertops

These are the areas you want to clean nearly last because you don't want to keep doing them over.

DAD *to* DAD

If you want to impress your wife with your bathroom-cleaning prowess, polish the fixtures with a used fabric softener sheet. Even better, the occasional use of chrome polish brightens up the room and makes it look as if you worked harder than you did.

1. Lightly dust the sink and countertops with cleanser. Dampen your sponge with warm water. Thoroughly scrub the inside and outside of the sink and the faucets, getting behind the taps and also around all the edges.

2. Wipe the wall behind the sink—a lot of stuff splatters here over the course of a week. Don't forget about the area where the soap is kept; even if it's in a removable soap dish, it gets gunked up. Soak up the soapy residue and rinse it away.

3. Rinse and squeeze out your sponge until no cleanser remains in it. Wet it again and go over all the areas you just wiped down, rinsing the sponge as necessary.

4. Lightly spritz the mirror with glass cleaner or white vinegar and wipe with paper towels in a circular motion. Use a dry edge of your paper towel or a fresh one to wipe the bits of paper towel lint out of the corners of the mirror. Spritz the faucet and fixtures with the same cleaner and wipe dry for a quick "spit shine."

5. Lightly spray an all-purpose cleaner over any countertops and wipe with dry paper towels.

Mopping Up: Finish with the Floor

A paper towel is fine for spot-cleaning the floor now and then (especially near the edges of the tub, where dust collects in the spray that drips over the edge), but the whole floor needs a good sponge-mopping once a week because the dust and dampness and drips of soap, hairspray, and toothpaste build up quickly here. Relax, though. Unless you live in a palace—and if you do, why are *you* mopping the floor?—the bathroom has a small amount of floor space, so it's a quick job. Start by removing the rug, wastebasket, scale, and anything portable on the floor.

To get your bathroom floor clean, fill a basin with warm water and floor cleaner or a small squirt of dishwashing liquid. Start in the farthest corner and work your way to the door, rinsing and squeezing out the sponge mop into the bucket every few strokes. When you get to the end, lay a dry, absorbent towel

Rug vs. Mat

Even if you have a bathroom rug, you need a separate bathmat to absorb water from bathers, which will keep your rug and floor cleaner and drier. After use, it can be hung to dry over the shower rail or the edge of the tub and washed with a regular load of towels.

BATHROOM

under your feet and "skate" across the floor for a quick drying to make sure nobody slips.

Bathroom rugs with a heavy rubber backing are hard to wash and usually can't go in the dryer. (If you do have one, run it through a cold wash—and an extra spin cycle—and hang it over the clothesline or the shower rail to dry.) A cotton rug without backing is more absorbent and far more comfortable to walk on than acrylic. For those reasons, you may opt for a simple cotton bathroom rug, which can be tossed in the wash—and should be—every two weeks or so. Try to buy a weighty one with a thick pile, which is far less prone to slip across a tile floor. Don't wash your bathroom rug with anything else, however. A thick cotton rug tossed in with a load of towels or clothes can unbalance the load and give off an astonishing profusion of lint. Trust me, I know from experience that you'll think you tossed in a full box of tissues.

Man Against Moisture

The Mildew Menace

Mildew is a thin, black fungus that grows in moist conditions, which is why it will thrive in the bathroom if you let it. A ventilator fan is a good preventative—use it during and after every shower. If you don't have one, open the bathroom window; even in winter, crack it open for a couple of minutes after your shower. Once mildew starts to sprout—when you see those telltale black flecks in your grout or sniff a musty odor—it's time to snuff it out. You can use potent chemical cleaners like Tilex, but they aren't always necessary. I find that going at the tiles and grout with a hard-bristled scrub brush and a mixture of laundry detergent and warm water works just as well. Rinse the tiles well with the water, then wipe down with a solution of one cup liquid bleach in a gallon of warm water. (Wear rubber gloves for this job.) Bad mildew spots may require you to apply pure bleach with a cotton ball. Allow the bleach to stand for up to an hour, then rinse well.

Dad's Own Laundromat:

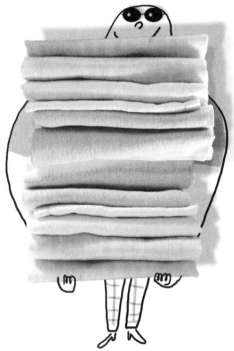

No More Pink T-shirts, Undies, or Briefs

If you can keep your family fed and dressed in clean clothes, you're functioning well, even if you haven't vacuumed under the bed in two months.

PRIORITY LEVEL:
High

NEEDS ATTENTION:
Weekly
(but with a baby or toddlers, could be daily)

LAUNDRY

For most dads, doing laundry is drudgery, but think about it: Washers and dryers are among the few appliances that really do save labor; you can drop in a fairly large load of clothing, spin the dial to "on," and walk away. As soon as that load goes into the dryer, you can start another load, which allows you to wash and dry hundreds—well, dozens, at least— of individual items of clothing in a couple of hours.

Taking a mountain of dirty clothes, returning them to a clean, fresh state, and putting them out of sight for another week gives me a real feeling of accomplishment. (Hey, you gotta take your rewards where you find them.)

In this chapter we'll cover laundry basics, like "pinkproof" sorting; Dad's own specialized stain removal—grass, chocolate, red wine, and especially cooking grease on the fronts of shirts—and folding, which, if done well, can eliminate the need for ironing. (And because sometimes you can't get out of it, ironing.)

Go with the Flow

With babies, laundry seems to happen every couple of hours, while with small kids, it's more like every couple of days. (If you don't have a washing machine or dryer and have to do your laundry somewhere else, check out page 85 for tips on Braving the Public Laundromat.) Older kids can be taught to do their own laundry, which may result in some shrinkage or nowhere-near-whites at first. But once they know what they're doing, think of all the time you'll save by not doing their laundry—and how they may even be able to start doing the rest of the family's wash.

It all comes down to need. You might need to wash a gym suit the night before a game, or do an

check out page 85 for tips on Braving the Public Laundromat.

DAD *to* **DAD**

As you're sorting through clothes, and before you start loading them into the machine, empty all pockets. You're going to make much more work for yourself if you accidentally wash a load of clothes with a pack of gum, or a Kleenex, or, heaven help us, a lipstick or crayon.

emergency wash on a pair of reeking sneakers. And now and then you'll find yourself rushing to the washing machine with a favorite white shirt that's been redecorated with ketchup or purple soda. There are lots of minor household crises that end at the washing machine, and the rate at your house will dictate how intimate you are with your spin cycles.

Laundry Sorting: A Beginner's Guide

Taking time to sort clothes carefully saves you a heap of headaches. Don't just assume that pile in the laundry hamper that looks white is all white. Flip through quickly and you may find a pair of red socks just waiting to turn your new briefs pink. Here are some fail-safe tips for laundry sorting:

1. Sort by color.

2. Sort by fabric type; no silk shirts with wool sweaters.

3. Separate heavily soiled clothes from the not-so-dirty stuff.

4. Read labels. Sometimes the most surprising items, like a spit-up-covered baby outfit, turn out to be "dry clean only."

5. When in doubt, don't. If you can't decide whether something is machine washable or dryer-safe, hand wash it and hang it out to dry or take it to the dry cleaner.

Standard sorting categories:

■ **Whites** All-white clothes only, such as underwear, crew socks, T-shirts.

■ **Darks** These include colored shirts and pants, which are then divided into heavy-duty cottons and jeans, and permanent press/synthetics and cotton/polyester blends.

■ **Linens** Fabrics you don't wear, like towels, washcloths, sheets, dish towels, and other items that might shed lint.

■ **Delicates and noncolorfast** Silks, acetates, lingerie, etc.

■ **Dry-clean-only** Suits and jackets, some shirts, some of your wife's skirts and dresses, certain wools, cashmere, suede, and velvet— always read the label.

■ **Unusual items**
Such as stuffed animals, pillows, sneakers, or down-filled vests, which all get washed on their own. (We'll talk about some special cases later.)

While you're sorting, look for grease spots, crayon marks, or other stains that you want to get out so they don't set permanently by a wash and dry. Treat these and other stains before you so much as spin a dial on the washing machine. Whenever possible, most stains should be treated as soon as they happen. See page 90 for Dad's Own Stain Guide, or use a commercial product such as those below.

Being Green: It's Not Always Easy

Clearly, I make a point of using as few industrial chemicals as possible around my kids. But commercial stain removers *are* quick. Homemade preparations are generally just as effective, but if you want to simply buy a stain remover, here are some nifty products (check manufacturer directions):

■ **Clorox Bleach Pen:** The angled tip and scrub brush allow you to apply bleach only to the stain, rather than to the whole garment.

■ **Tide to Go:** Another pen, primed with detergent, for application to stains when you're on the go. It will prevent them from setting in.

■ **Spray 'n Wash/Zout/Shout/Oxy-Foam, etc.:** All products for home use that you spray, squirt, or rub onto garments to help remove stains; best when applied right after the stain occurs. Many of these are also available as individually wrapped wipes for dabbing on clothes when you're away from home.

■ **Natural enzymes:** Bi-O-Kleen's Bac-Out is a very effective stain cleaner with enzymes that help digest the proteins in stains such as blood and baby spit-up.

Don't forget one last weapon in the fight against stains: your computer. Searching for stain removal sites or advice on specific stains pulls up a huge variety of helpful options.

■ *Linens* (towels and sheets, not linen fabric) are washed in a warm normal cycle, although light-colored linens can be washed hot if they're especially dirty.

■ *Delicates* should always be washed in cold water on the gentle cycle and, preferably, inside a lingerie bag (see sidebar below).

Lock and Load

Before you drop the first item of clothing into your washer, start it up, let the water rise, and then swish the detergent into the water. Doing this ensures that you

Laundry Prep Precautions

Zippers, snaps, hooks, buttons, and other fasteners have a way of grabbing onto other laundry, riddling it with snags, and loosening themselves in the process. Also, certain fabrics were born to collect lint and will if left to their own devices. To keep clothes from snagging, to avoid having certain clothes look like they just came from a tickertape parade, and to avoid having to replace buttons (Dads generally don't consider sewing part of their job description), follow these tips before you wash:

■ Snap or hook all lingerie items and, ideally, wash them in a lingerie bag (a small mesh laundry bag—your wife probably already owns one, but till now you didn't know what it was for) to prevent excess wear and snagging. A bra hook can shred a pair of hose faster and more thoroughly than a food processor shreds a carrot.

■ Button and zip all pants and turn them inside out to reduce fading and prevent brass studs and zippers from rubbing against other clothes.

■ Turn washable velvets, corduroy, and anything black inside out. This protects the pile in velvet; the other two are lint magnets.

■ It's *not* necessary to button ordinary polo-neck shirts or dress shirts *unless* your dress shirts or your wife's blouses have special tailored details such as raised mother-of-pearl buttons. If so, fasten the buttons and turn the shirt inside out to prevent them from tearing loose.

LAUNDRY

don't overfill the washer with clothes and that your liquid or powdered detergent is evenly distributed throughout the water. Don't pour detergent right onto your clothes, as it has been known to leave spots. Don't risk ruining your wife's favorite silk camisole or your six-year-old's favorite shirt—in the universe of Dad housekeeping, it's the beloved item that will get the weird detergent spots.

Put clothes in after you've added detergent, but remember, just because you *can* cram in every single shred of clothing doesn't mean you should. Clothes should be loosely packed and fill only about half the drum. Tightly packed clothes can't move around in the soapy water and therefore don't get as clean. (Pack them too tightly and not all of them will even get completely *wet.*)

Once all the clothes are loaded, close the lid and let the machine go about its business. Most washing machines take approximately half an hour to run.

Laundry 411

1. *Less is more.* And that goes for both detergent and fabric softener. Too much soap doesn't get things cleaner; it makes the water too sudsy and actually prevents dirt from being lifted away. Extra soap can also cling to the fibers and attract dirt to the item more quickly. Too much fabric softener will make clothes feel almost sticky. It's also not good to wash infants' clothes with fabric softener because their skin is very sensitive to chemicals and scents. Stick with a pediatrician-recommended detergent, like Dreft, which gently cleans and also softens.

2. *Front-loading washers are better.* It's not just because they lock and you can't reopen them until the cycle is done. Front loaders are more efficient, using far less energy and water, and experts say that they are much gentler on your clothes, keeping them "newer" longer. What's more, because they use a relatively small amount of water, they require about one-third the detergent top loaders need. (By the way, lots of major brands now have "HE," or "high-efficiency," versions of detergents to prevent excess sudsing in front-loading washers.)

3. *Be gentle.* Washing clothes causes fading, but not necessarily because the dye washes out. When you always wash on the "Heavy" or "Cotton" setting and use water that's too hot, your blues and blacks get agitated and spun harder and the roughened surfaces go gray faster. For a lightly soiled load, try the gentle cycle and cooler water.

Braving the Public Laundromat

Don't have a washer-dryer? Nothing can be worse than facing a busy Laundromat, especially when you have a family's worth of dirty clothes to get done. Try to stay upbeat. Remind yourself of how much laundry you can do at one time—you've reduced your wash days to one or two a week. And even though you're popping quarters as if you were at the slot machines in Vegas, remember what you're *not* spending on utility bills. Here are some ways to stay sane while getting your family's clothes clean:

■ Be at the Laundromat when it opens so you can claim the washers you want. Your clothes should be done before anyone else's, which means you'll also have first dibs on the dryers. Avoid Saturday and Sunday afternoons and evenings like the plague. Doing laundry at off hours, like a Wednesday afternoon, will mean fewer people to fight for the machines.

■ Transport your liquid supplies in small containers. Just because you saved money on value-size jugs doesn't mean you need to throw your back out lugging them.

■ Check on clothes before the time runs out in the dryer and pull out the items that are already dry, like sheets and underwear. It will be easier for the rest of the clothes to get dry and means less wear and tear on all your laundry.

LAUNDRY

Washing Loveys

If you have a young child, chances are he or she has a "lovey"—a stuffed animal, doll, or blankie that the child can't live without. Loveys get truly filthy because children take them everywhere.

How you get the lovey away from your child is not the least of your problems. I tell my son that he and Daddy are going to clean his puppy together. I let him stand on a stool by the washer and help me add the detergent. If it's really hard to separate lovey from child, wait till he is sleeping and quietly borrow the lovey for a nighttime stealth washing. (Just make sure you slide it back before morning!)

LAUNDRY

If toys don't have specific washing instructions, the ones below will see you safely through.

For stuffed animals and toys with cloth parts only

1. Use cold water and mild liquid detergent on the delicate cycle.

2. Add a clean bath towel to the wash to help rub the toy clean.

3. Depending on how delicate the toy is, you may want to skip the spin cycle. Instead, gently squeeze the toy free of water, without twisting, and either hang it on the line in the sun or suspend it over a tub or sink where it can drip dry.

4. Most loveys that say they're not washable can survive a machine wash, but if the toy is overloved or delicate, don't risk disintegration. Instead, fill a basin with a gallon of cold water, a squeeze of dish liquid, and ¼ cup of baking soda. Swish the lovey around in there, then leave it to soak awhile. Gently scrub really dirty spots with a toothbrush, and rinse in cold water. Squeeze very gently (no twisting) and set it on a towel to dry, turning the toy over every few hours.

For toys with some cloth parts and some plastic or metal

1. If the lovey comes apart, such as a cloth-bodied doll whose plastic head can be removed, you may be able to wash the cloth part in the machine separately—just don't let your child watch the decapitation. Scrub the plastic or metal parts with a damp sponge and a little baking soda, rinse well with a clean sponge, and dry on a towel.

2. If the parts are inseparable, use a damp sponge dipped in baking soda to wipe the noncloth parts, then a sponge dipped in warm water with a squirt of dish soap to clean the cloth parts. Scrub gently with a clean toothbrush as needed, rinse well, and dry on a towel.

■ Don't be cheap. Spread your clothes among as many dryers as you can without being lynched by your fellow washers. The less you have in each dryer, the less time it will take to dry. What you save on quarters in cramming a single dryer full, you'll make up for when you have to keep feeding the dryer until everything's done. And you're saving on wear and tear.

■ If you don't live too far from the Laundromat (as in, you can be home in less than five minutes), pack dry clothes neatly in the laundry bag and fold them at home. When you get in, drape dry clothes flat over furniture to keep them crease-free. Take advantage of little hands to make the work lighter. Kids can easily fold pillow cases, napkins, placemats, paired socks, and other uncomplicated items.

So Many Detergents, So Little Time

Nowadays, deciding between liquid and powder is only the beginning. A single brand like Tide has 15 varieties to choose from. What's a Dad to do? Here are the only things you need to know about laundry soaps:

■ **Powdered detergents** are more economical and are better at removing mud, dirt, and children's stains.

■ **Liquid detergents** are better at pre-treating and at removing protein stains and grease.

■ **Brighteners:** These fluorescents leave a residue to keep colors bright. They're harder on skin, the environment, and clothes.

■ **Fragrances/dyes:** Perfumes irritate kids' skin and dye is purely cosmetic. Try a "free" detergent, without scent or dye additives. Biodegradable, "green" detergents are effective and safe.

■ **Softeners:** It's best to use a plain detergent and add fabric softener separately so that clothes like towels and dishtowels don't get softener residue, which makes them less absorbent.

■ **Enzymes:** Potent enzymes clean biological and food stains but are tough on the environment, so save them only for clothes that really need them.

Washing Weird Stuff

Things besides everyday clothes and linens can and do go into the wash, but launder them by themselves with these directions:

■ **Sneakers:** Canvas sneakers with rubber or plastic soles can be unlaced and tossed in the machine on a warm cycle. Be sure shoes are fully air-dried. Unlace all other sneakers, remove inserts, and scrub shoe with a soft brush, warm water, and dishwashing liquid. A stain-erasing sponge gets scuffs off leather or plastic. (Check online for manufacturer's instructions on washing.)

■ **Bed and Throw Pillows:** Remove pillow covers and slips before washing. Put polyester and down pillows in the machine, two per load, and wash gently in warm water. Tumble-dry on low with a couple of tennis balls to fluff them up.

■ **Down- or Polyester-Filled Vests and Coats:** Follow manufacturer's instructions, but most can be safely washed in a gentle cold or warm cycle and dried with a clean sneaker or tennis balls, as above.

Dad's All-Purpose Spray 'n Leave

This recipe is as effective as any general stain treatment. The secret is to get it on the stain *fast.*

  1 quart water
  ¼ cup white vinegar
  ¼ cup baking soda
  ¼ cup dishwashing liquid (preferably a degreasing type, such as Dawn)

Blend (don't shake) the ingredients in a clean spray bottle. Wait till the foam subsides completely, then cap and label clearly.

After spraying, rub it into the stain, then roll the item around the wet spot and leave it for up to . . . well, I've left things up to a week before washing.

Dad's Own Stain Guide

Because I think like a Dad, I like to be as low-tech as possible when it comes to stain removal. Most industrial-strength stain cleaners contain highly potent or potentially toxic chemicals, so I use them only as a last resort. I don't want them running through my septic tank, and I certainly don't want my kids getting into or inhaling them or wearing their residue.

The secret to stain removal is speed: When you see something serious, such as grape juice or mustard, spill on you or your child, move as fast as possible. (If you're worried about the item of clothing, that is. My older son has a striped blue-and-white shirt that has Technicolor food and paint stains down the front, but it's still his favorite and I've long since given up trying to get it stain-free.)

Note: All the suggestions in this stain chart are intended only for *machine-washable fabrics and NOT for silk, wool, acetate, or acrylic.* Because of the harmless nature of most of these sprays or scrubs, you may be able to use them on, say, a wool sweater, but do a spot test first on an interior area such as a seam.

Low-Tech Stain Removers

These safe solvents along with an extra shot of laundry detergent can clean most stains:

- white vinegar
- lemon juice
- baking soda
- salt
- club soda or seltzer

These bigger guns are also relatively harmless chemicals:

- rubbing alcohol
- glycerin
- hydrogen peroxide
- ammonia
- borax
- chlorine bleach

LAUNDRY

STAIN	ANTIDOTE
Biological Stains BABY FORMULA MILK (BREASTMILK, TOO) MEAT JUICE EGG	Scrape off excess, wet with cold water. Mix 1 cup dishwasher liquid, 1 cup ammonia, 1 cup water in a spray bottle. Saturate stain, scrub with toothbrush until stain fades (applying more remover as needed), then launder immediately.
Blood	Pour hydrogen peroxide onto stain, let bubble and foam, add more liquid until stain fades, rinse, and then launder in cold water. For leather or suede, dab lightly with hydrogen peroxide and wipe with lint-free cloth.
Cloth Diapers	Rinse in cool water to remove solids (most parents do this in the toilet). Presoak in machine with 1 cup white vinegar in warm water. Wash stubborn loads in hot water with 1 cup borax.
Dirt and Mud	Scrape off excess. Wet with cold water and rub in bar soap or laundry detergent. Scrub with a firm brush, rinsing and repeating until stain is gone.
Foods BANANA CHOCOLATE ICE CREAM JAM AND JELLY KETCHUP AND TOMATO SAUCE	For any of these food stains, use Dad's Spray 'n Leave formula (page 89). After scraping off excess, wet with water and saturate with Spray 'n Leave. Let sit and then launder as usual.
Furniture Polish **Motor Oil** INDUSTRIAL GREASE OR OIL	Spray with a shot of WD-40, Go-Jo, or Permatex, scrub lightly, let sit for half an hour, wash out with dishwashing liquid, and launder separately in hot water.

LAUNDRY

STAIN	ANTIDOTE (cont'd)
Glue	For serious adhesives, dab with rubbing alcohol or acetone nail-polish remover in a ventilated area. (Never use on acrylic or acetate.)
Grease and Oils BUTTER SALAD DRESSING COSMETICS CRAYON DEODORANT AND PERSPIRATION	Mix 2 cups water, 1/4 cup glycerin, 1/4 cup concentrated dishwashing liquid in a glass bottle or jar and keep on hand for these tough stains. Saturate, scrub with a toothbrush, let sit for a day, and wash in hot water.
Gum	Rub with ice cube to freeze gum and remove excess, saturate with white vinegar, let sit for 15 to 20 minutes, and with fingertip rub up the remains.
Ink and Ballpoint Pen	Saturate with hair spray, scrub, rinse with cold water, repeat until stain is nearly gone. Dip in pigment stain remover (opposite page) and wash.
Mildew and Mold	Mix 2 tbs. vinegar into 1 cup milk, then saturate mildew stains. Dry in sunlight, then wash in warm water.
Old, Set-in Grease Stains	Dampen with cold water and apply a big squirt of Dawn grease-cutting dishwashing liquid. Rub in well, allow to sit for at least an hour, launder warm or hot.
Poop	Scrape off excess, rinse with cool water. Scrub with bar soap, rubbing fabric together, and rinse with warm water. For persistent stains, treat with 1 tbs. hydrogen peroxide and 1 tbs. dishwashing liquid in 1/2 cup warm water.
Red Wine	Immediately rinse with club soda or white wine. Sprinkle liberally with salt and scrub in cold water, rubbing the stain out.

STAIN	ANTIDOTE (cont'd)
Rust	Spritz stain with lemon juice, sprinkle with salt, and scrub with a toothbrush. Allow lemon juice to sit on stain for several hours for mild bleaching action before washing.
Staining Pigments BERRIES COFFEE JUICE MUSTARD ORANGE, RED, OR PURPLE SODA	When possible, douse with seltzer or club soda to prevent setting. Wet with cold water, then mix 1 tbs. white vinegar, 1 tbs. milk, 2 tsp. lemon juice, 1 tsp. borax, 1 tsp. salt in a bowl. Dip the stained spot in the bowl and scrub with a toothbrush. Rinse with cold water, repeat until stain fades.
Stickers and Tape	Pull off excess, wet with warm water, and rub with dishwashing liquid (works for water-based adhesives). Or rub with baby oil or glycerin, scrub with a toothbrush, wash with dishwashing liquid and warm water, and launder as usual.
Urine	For a child's "accident," wash as usual as soon as possible. For pet urine or a stain that has dried, prevent lingering odor by treating with 1 tbs. dishwashing liquid and 1 tbs. white vinegar in 1 cup warm water. Rinse with warm water and launder as usual.
Wax	Let wax solidify, scrape off as much excess as possible, place a sheet of brown paper or a brown paper bag over wax, gently iron area until wax melts and soaks into paper—about 30 seconds. Move paper to fresh spot and repeat as necessary.

LAUNDRY

Know How to Fold It

I feel about clothes folding the way I do about dish drying: There is entirely too much of it going on. Here are a few things to remember.

The point of folding clothes is to smooth them for storage—and to avoid ironing! But when I took charge of the laundry, I wasn't about to be cowed by housekeeping experts who apparently have a lot more time on their hands to make perfect squares out of fitted sheets than I have. So I came up with a new system. Once you get everyone in the family on board, you'll see how much easier my system is— and how much smoother it leaves your clothes.

Part I: Hang Everything Possible

■ Take synthetic shirts out of the dryer just before they're dry and place them on hangers so they don't have time to crease. Works for some poly/cotton blends, too.

■ As you pull clothes out of the dryer, lay them as flat as possible in the laundry basket instead of just letting them clump at will.

■ If you can't fold laundry immediately,

drape it as flat as possible over the couch or a few chairs. Leaving it crammed in the laundry basket is asking for wrinkles.

If you have room in your closets, hang all pants, even jeans. You can fold them with or without a crease down the leg, then lay them over a hanger and put it away. I usually do creases on the fronts of khakis and dress pants, but fold jeans in half without a front crease.

Hang all button-front shirts on a hanger and button top or middle button. Ditto for blouses and jackets. (Plastic hangers are best because they don't leave lines.) Don't hang T-shirts, sweaters, or knit shirts or you'll get little raised pockmarks in the shoulders.

Part II: Never Fold Underwear Again

Don't fold the small stuff, or fold it as minimally as possible. Socks need to be paired, but that's accomplished by flipping over a small cuff at the top of each pair. There's no need to turn one inside out within the other.

Underwear large and small should be stacked flat, one pair on top of the next (this was the breakthrough that led me to everything else). Lay the stack flat in your underwear drawer. It won't take up more room than it did when rolled or quartered because now you can build it much higher. Best of all, because the stacks are wider, they will be less likely to topple over, which always happens with my small folded stacks.

Bras and lingerie receive the slightest touch (if any): Just fold them in half. Fold tights or stockings vertically like pants and then horizontally at the knee.

Baby clothes, when small, can be laid flat in stable stacks of flat onesies, T-shirts, and little pants rather than in toppling quartered towers.

Part III: Think Like a Store Manager

I've never worked at Gap, but I've shopped at plenty, which is how I got the idea for my T-shirt fold. Most department stores do it this way, too.

Forget the fancy maneuver that requires you to fold the T-shirt in thirds lengthwise and then in half. Instead, fold the sleeves, short or long, across the back

LAUNDRY

of the shirt, then fold
the whole shirt in half
crosswise and stack
it. You'll have a large,
smooth rectangle of
shirts with only one
horizontal fold.

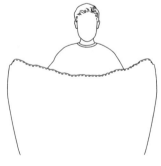

Sweaters, jerseys, and
knit shirts get folded like
T-shirts: two arms behind,
then halved across the
middle. Your clothes will
look smoother and your
effort will be, well, halved.

The same rule applies
to pants if you don't have
room to hang them. Look at
a display pile of khakis in a
clothing store. Chances are, they're folded in half
with front pocket facing front pocket, then folded
once crosswise at the knee. This fold, too, takes up
more surface area but can be laid in deeper, more
stable stacks.

Don't be a slave to sheets, pillowcases, towels,
washcloths, cloth napkins, and tablecloths. Do the
quickest, largest fold that you have room to store. I
lay washcloths flat on top of one another; pillowcases
are halved.

Grasp a fitted
sheet by the inner
edges of the corner
seams and fold it
in half widthwise,
tucking one corner
inside its opposite.
Quarter the sheet,
then halve and
quarter it again. The
gathered ends may
hang out a bit, but it
will roughly square up
as you fold. You won't
have a perfect, square
package like you would
if you'd spent half an

hour tucking in the gathered ends
of the sheet, but you're a dad and
don't have time for that kind of
obsessive folding.

Iron Man

The key to ironing is to do it as rarely as humanly
possible. Things that need pressing at my house—
such as, perhaps, my wife's suits—go to the dry

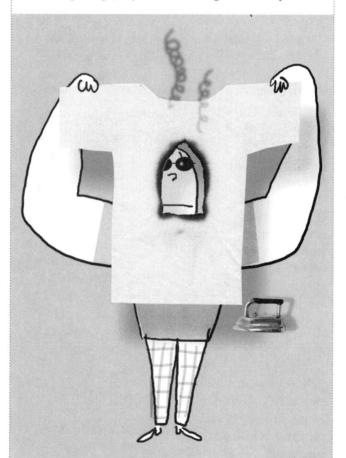

Salvaging Scorched Clothes

For a slight scorch, place a clean wet cloth over the
item and rerun the iron over it. You can also rub the
scorch mark lightly with white vinegar, then wipe with a
clean cloth. Treat more intense marks with 1 part water
to 1 part hydrogen peroxide or a solution of ¼ cup
borax to 1 quart water. Rinse thoroughly.

LAUNDRY

cleaner. For those rare occasions when you find yourself in the unfortunate position of having to iron, here are a few things to keep in mind:

■ Unplug the iron before filling it with water.

■ Read the fabric guide (usually printed right on the iron) to gauge the right temperature. Acetate, nylon, acrylic, and silk are dry ironed on low heat; polyester, wool, cotton, and linen are steam ironed on higher heat.

■ Use the wide end of the ironing board for large items, like sheets, tablecloths, and the bodies of shirts, and the small, pointy end for intricate tasks like the tops of pants or the collars and sleeves of shirts.

■ Iron the underside of a shirt collar first and the front will get ironed out at the same time.

■ Lay creased pants flat with leg seams aligned on top of each other. Iron the outside of the top leg first. Then lay that leg over the top of the pants and iron the inner part of the other leg. Flip the pants over and repeat.

■ For creases you want to keep or make (down the front of pants, or pleats), place parchment or brown paper on either side of the crease and iron on top of the paper.

■ If you must iron woolens, lay a moistened white tea towel over the fabric and use a hot iron. Make sure the wool is lying flat under the cloth.

■ To prevent delicate clothes from scorching, place a cloth or towel between the garment and the iron (especially useful for delicate fabrics like linen or nylon).

■ **Never** leave the iron unattended when it's on.

■ When you're done, unplug the iron and put it and the cord out of reach of curious little hands.

The Comfort Zone:

Family Rooms

For some, the living room and family room are the same. In these rooms, families spend their downtime. It's where

PRIORITY LEVEL:
Medium

NEEDS CLEANING:
At least once a week

they relax and take out their toys, whether that's a DVD player or a choo-choo. In my family, it only takes a few hours for the family room to look like a bomb hit.

FAMILY ROOMS:

5 Minute Attack

You Will Need:

**MICROFIBER OR COTTON CLOTHS
(OLD T-SHIRTS ARE GOOD)
PAPER TOWELS
FURNITURE WAX OR POLISH
GLASS CLEANER OR VINEGAR
DUST MOP OR SWIFFER
VACUUM**

Tidy the Tables

2 MINUTES

■ Remove schoolbooks, forgotten drinking glasses, clothing—anything that doesn't belong in the room.

■ Neatly stack magazines, remote controls, and books on the coffee table.

■ Put DVDs, CDs, or video games back in their cases.

■ Gather toys off the floor and fling them in a toy box or basket (I keep a wicker laundry basket in the family room for speedy cleanups).

Clean the Floors

2 MINUTES

■ Run the vacuum over high-traffic areas and all rugs. Use the dust mop or Swiffer to gather up the dust bunnies and dust rhinos on uncarpeted floors.

Finishing Touches

1 MINUTE

■ Fluff up furniture cushions and fold any blankets or artfully drape them on the back of the sofa.

■ With a microfiber cloth, dust the coffee and end tables. If you're feeling ambitious, spray the tops with glass cleaner or furniture polish, whichever is appropriate, and wipe clean with a cloth or paper towel.

Besides managing the clutter in these spaces, there's vacuuming, sometimes mopping, and, yes, dusting. (All these techniques also apply to your dining room, which should be vacuumed and dusted once a week.) In this chapter we'll look at ways to keep these rooms habitable and moderately tidy, including ways your family can help with daily maintenance.

Family Functions

Just like the kitchen and bathroom, everyday rooms require some everyday maintenance. But that doesn't have to mean it's all up to you. If you train your family members to pick up as they go, the weekly overhaul will be that much easier to tackle, so it's worth putting in the time to make sure they do their part. Daily upkeep:

■ If your family is allowed to eat in the living room, make it a rule that they take their own dishes and glasses to the kitchen when they're finished.

■ Keep a cordless, handheld vacuum cleaner, such as a DustBuster or Shark, in these rooms to vacuum up crumbs.

■ When shoes or socks come off, the owner must take them with her when she leaves the room and put them where they belong.

■ Once you've finished with a newspaper or magazine (and made sure your wife is also done with it), put it in a "recycle" pile. Take the pile out when you leave the room for the night.

■ Consider placing a small bookcase, with a shelf for each family member, at the entrance. Everyone should put their things, like reading materials, toys, etc., on their respective shelves when finished using them. Things that belong in the bedroom should go back to the bedroom.

The Weekly Family Room Clean

You will need

- microfiber dustcloths

- furniture cleaner (Endust, for instance)

- glass cleaner

- paper towels

- white vinegar, if you prefer the natural route

- vacuum cleaner, with attachments, for upholstery, carpets, curtains, and radiators

- broom, dust mop, or Swiffer

- sponge mop, for washing floors

- bucket or basin

- dry sponge, for removing pet hair

How to Vacuum

Vacuuming is a task few people enjoy, but it's the quickest, most efficient way to clean your floors. For the most part, you can concentrate on high-traffic areas, but once a week you need to be more thorough.

Before you vacuum, scan the floor for small, hard objects, like paper clips, coins, and tiny toys, and pick them up. These can stop up the vacuum hose or even break the motor. Put small items like knitting baskets and magazine racks, even lightweight chairs, on top of tables or outside the room. Move portable furniture like tables and chairs before you vacuum. (Save vacuuming under heavy stuff like the couch for a monthly chore.)

What's in a Vac?

Your vacuum cleaner is something you'll use at least weekly, and if pets or family members have asthma or allergies, it could be daily. The vacuum business has boomed in recent years, and this boring old workhorse of an appliance has become a chic designer tool. Because style doesn't equal power, it's really worth searching the Internet (try Epinions.com) to find out what other buyers are saying about the model that interests you. Here are the basic types of vacuums available:

■ **Upright vacuums** These bulky vacuum cleaners work best when you're dealing with wall-to-wall plush carpeting, but most of them do come with attachments (see page 107) that make them useful for cleaning bare floors as well as curtains and drapes. Newer upright models often come with attachments that essentially convert the machine to a handheld. Upright vacuums have come a long way, in terms of both design and effectiveness, and there's one in every price range. If you still have an old cumbersome model, go shopping now.

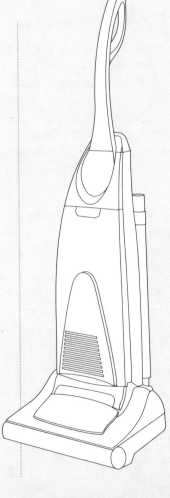

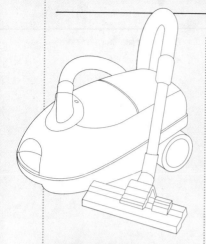

■ Ultralight-weight vacuums (ULW)

ULWs are uprights that weigh only about eight pounds. Depending on the model, they can work just as well as standard upright or canister vacuums, but they usually have no attachments and can't be used to clean bare floors.

■ Canister vacuums

Canisters are maneuverable, which means they're really great for cleaning hard-to-reach spots (under and around furniture legs, for instance) and also nonfloor surfaces (sofa cushions, upholstery, curtains). And since you don't need to do any conversions to add the attachments, they're simpler to work with. They also tend to be the priciest type of vacuum, but a quality one, such as the Swedish brand Electrolux, can last a lifetime.

HEPA or Nothing

If anyone in your family suffers from dust allergies or asthma, you should be using a vacuum with a HEPA (High-Efficiency Particulate Air) filter. My HEPA vac, an upright Hoover I bought for $79 on sale, does not have a replaceable bag but runs through a filter into a chamber that can be emptied. However, if you have a mold problem, buy a higher-end HEPA vac with a disposable bag—they're better at trapping mold spores, a common and aggressive allergen.

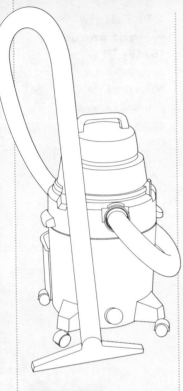

■ Electric brooms

Think of the electric broom as the "go-cart" of the vacuum family—in other words, handy, but not the vehicle you can rely on. When they work, power brooms are great for quickies (e.g., to give a hardwood floor a once-over). But they're also pretty cheap, so don't expect a lot of power, durability, or reliability.

■ Wet-dry vacs

These used to be called shopvacs because they were designed for rough work only. Now you can get fancy wet-dry vacs for home use, both for cleaning wet carpets and for sucking up wet messes. Many come with washable filters for ease of use. Because strong suction is important, look for a model with the highest amps you can afford.

■ Handheld vacuums

These small vacs are great for quick jobs such as sucking up spilled popcorn. Some need to be plugged in, others are cordless and rechargeable, and Scünci even makes a handheld, cordless wet-dry vac. Prices and quality are all over the map, so check around before you buy.

What the Heck Are All Those Parts For?

If you're like I used to be, you probably don't know a vacuum cleaner even has attachments, much less what to do with them.

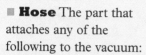

■ **Hose** The part that attaches any of the following to the vacuum:

■ **Bare-floor brush** For bare floors, including hardwood, tile, stone, linoleum, and others. Replace as soon as the brush part gets worn.

■ **Rug-cleaning tool** A special device for low-pile carpets and worn rugs.

■ **Power nozzle** For thick carpets and sturdy rugs.

■ **Crevice tool** Used for edges and baseboards and also good between sofa cushions and radiator fins and along window tracks and carpet edges. Just wipe clean after each use.

■ **Upholstery tool** Used to vacuum couches, chairs, and other upholstered furniture, as well as curtains, drapes, and stairs. To dust delicate furnishings, cover the tool with a soft, clean cloth.

■ **Dusting brush** To brush away cobwebs that collect in corners on the ceiling, as well as baseboards, blinds, shutters, pictures, books, and bookcases. Wield it gently when you're dealing with anything delicate, like lighting fixtures or framed pictures.

■ **Wand** Extension rod between the hose and the attachments. Check it occasionally to clear obstructions.

FAMILY ROOMS

Which Comes First?

It's a common dilemma: Do you dust first or vacuum first? It depends on who you ask. My advice: Experiment with what works for you. If you find that dusting last is mucking up the carpet or that your vacuum cleaner has a tendency to create dust, switch the order.

As you vacuum, use long strokes and pull backward over areas you've vacuumed a couple of times. Try to overlap your strokes so you don't miss any sections. Most important, Dads, look at what you are vacuuming, so you see dirt you missed or things that need special attention—like the areas in front of couches and chairs.

You can easily shampoo high-traffic areas and problem spots (pet stains, for example), using one of the foaming carpet shampoos available in the supermarket. Simply spray the foam on the carpet, let it soak in according to manufacturer's directions, and vacuum away. There's no need to shampoo unless there are actual stains, but if you do have a food spill or a pet accident, shampoo quickly before the stain dries and sets. If you don't catch it quickly, you may need to call in a professional or rent a steam-clean vac.

And remember, you're a guy—don't sprinkle or spray vacuum-able "carpet freshener" on your floors. For one thing, men aren't really into perfumed fresheners, and for another, your kids don't need to inhale the residue into their growing lungs.

Besides cleaning your floors, vacuuming is a great way to help keep dust at bay. Every month or so, vacuum your upholstery and drapes as well as your carpets, using the upholstery tool and dusting brush attachments (see page 107). If your vacuum cleaner did not come with attachments, you may want to invest in an inexpensive lightweight or handheld vacuum to do these tasks. Suction makes the task much simpler.

The last thing to remember is to clean out your vacuum regularly so that it works properly. Bags should be changed before they get too full or you risk an explosion. (Take a peek at the bag after each vacuuming session.) With bagless models, the removable residue catcher should be emptied when it's half full or whenever you've finished vacuuming the whole house. Just check the chamber occasionally, especially if you have pets.

Beyond the Vacuum

If you don't have carpeting or rugs in your living room or family room, you still have to get the floor clean. You must sweep or vacuum any floor type before you wash it. Otherwise you end up with a lot of wet dust and dirt and a not-very-clean floor. If you're sweeping, debris goes in a dustpan—not behind the door or under the rug.

If your dustpan is dented or bent at the edge, replacing it will make the task much less frustrating. Buy a dustpan with a thin rubber edge that will lie flat against an uneven floor.

Wood is one of the most common floor types for the living room. It looks really elegant when treated well, but if you don't keep spots and food off it, it will start to look ratty. There are lots of commercial floor products, but I prefer the natural route, mixing a cup of vinegar into a bucket of warm water for basic floor cleaning. When it comes to bad scuffs or other spots, essential oils really do the trick. A drop of lemon or orange essential oil rubbed into the spot will take it right out. Tea tree oil works very well for light-wood floors; so does lavender oil mixed with a drop of lemon juice, and it smells like the real thing, not a fake chemical scent.

Real wood floors might warp if they're wet for too long, so once your floor is washed, dry it immediately. Use the "skating" technique: After washing the floor, lay down a clean, absorbent towel. Step on the towel and slide across the floor as if you were skating. (You might need a couple of old towels if you have lots of bare floor.)

If you want to prevent floors in doorways from getting worn spots, apply a light coat of paste wax

DAD *to* DAD

When you sweep, spray your broom or dust mop with Endust or even a light spritz of furniture polish so the dust doesn't leap all over the room.

with a soft cloth once a month and allow the wax to dry for 15 minutes or so. Give it a quick buff with a clean dry mop, then wait an hour and repeat. And to quick-shine any floor between waxings, mop the floor with your dustmop or Swiffer. (If you don't have a Swiffer, get one; they make cleaning floors and furniture much, much easier.)

Real Men *Do* Dust

But that doesn't mean we like it. No doubt about it: Dusting is boring. Luckily, there are ways to avoid having to do it more than once a week (although you should do it about that often). Prevention is your best line of defense. If you keep your windows closed, you can keep most of the dust out of your house. But who's going to do that? Another option is to cover your windows with allergy-protector screens.

An old, *clean* tube sock rolled over your hand makes a great "dusting glove," especially when you're trying to get into crevices that require a little more dexterity than an open dust cloth can provide. You can also look for microfiber gloves, which collect dust like magic. Here are some ways to get the job done quickly, efficiently, and effectively:

■ For best results, start at the top of the room and work your way down.

■ Ceiling fans are dust magnets. Try wiping them off with a microfiber cloth.

■ Remember to run your dust cloth over *all* surfaces, including those hard-to-reach chair legs and backs of ladder- or spoke-back chairs.

■ Don't forget about lighting fixtures, ceiling vents, floor vents, and doors. The best way to dust these is to break out the vacuum. Connect the dusting brush attachment to an extension wand

---

DAD *to* DAD

Real men dust with microfiber. These cloths have 200,000 strands per square inch, and they're nonabrasive and lint-free. They generate their own electromagnetic charge to attract dust, pick up 90% of bacteria, and can be washed and reused.

(see page 107) and suck the dust away.

■ Dust lamp shades with a clean microfiber cloth. Use your fingertip to work it into pleats. You can also try using a lint roller on a smooth shade or simply vacuum with the upholstery attachment.

■ If you have silk flowers or plastic plants in your home, bring out the hair dryer. There's no reason to wipe these sometimes delicate, always-too-intricate surfaces clean when you can blow your troubles away.

■ Don't bother dusting sturdy knickknacks or some display plates, vases, and like items; many of these can go in the dishwasher. (Don't put them in there with anything else and make sure they're well seated.)

Furniture Polish: Don't Believe the Hype

Do you really need to polish your furniture every week? Depends on what type of polish you use. Some are designed to fade quickly, requiring frequent reapplication. Before you wipe another tabletop, check out these categories of polish:

■ **Emulsion polishes** These have a milky look when applied and are mainly a mix of oil and water. They're good for cleaning—but no better than a damp, soapy rag.

■ **Furniture oils** These are often scented with citrus oils, but mainly they contain mineral oil, which gives a very shiny surface that fades quickly while still attracting dirt and dust.

■ **Silicone polishes** Check the ingredients list. Many popular

> ### DAD *to* DAD
>
> **T**o clean wood furniture, use a wood cleaner like Murphy Oil Soap. Follow up with a fresh coat of paste wax if you want a super shine.

polishes contain silicone to give a high sheen that will last longer than oil, but they make it very difficult to refinish the furniture since the residue will prevent the new finish from sticking.

■ **Paste waxes** Wax is the way to go for a deep, rich glow that doesn't attract dirt. Even better, it should last three to six months. Look for a beeswax paste such as Briwax. Apply a thin layer, allow to dry for 20 minutes, then buff to a high gloss with a clean cotton cloth and lots of elbow grease. Afterward, you need to dust only occasionally with a microfiber rag or wipe with a wet cloth if the item is dirty.

Fast Furniture Fixes

When it comes to furniture, wear and tear is inevitable. It's also inevitable that your kids, guests, or even you and your wife will find a way to damage good furniture, especially, it seems, if it was pricey. Most things you knick, dent, burn, or stain can be repaired, though. Here's how:

■ If you clean spots and stains as they happen, before they set, chances are better that you'll be able to get them out.

■ If something wet has spilled on your couch, *blot it*—whatever you do, DON'T RUB IT IN or you'll only spread the stain.

■ For a dry spot, loosen the caked-on crud with your hand, a fingernail, or the edge of a credit card, then vacuum the spot to get up the smaller debris before you use any kind of cleaning solution or even water on the area.

■ Always pretest a cleaning solution by applying it to an inconspicuous area of the furniture. Five minutes later, rub that area with an old towel. If the color from the material shows up on the towel, try another product. (We'll go into more detail on cleaning furniture in the Spring Cleaning chapter.)

■ Use a white cloth when removing stains from furniture—you never know when something's going to run color.

■ After using a cleaning product, rinse the cleaned area thoroughly, as the product can actually attract dirt.

■ Dilute cleansers according to the manufacturer's directions. Too strong a solution won't get the job done better—you'll just wear out your couch faster.

■ "Scrub" pet hair off furniture with a dry, new—that means never-used—sponge.

Remove chewing gum from carpets, curtains, or upholstery by rubbing an ice cube on it until it hardens. Then scrape off the hardened gum with your finger.

Spritz a little hairspray on a ballpoint ink stain and let it stand for a minute or so. Be sure to rinse the area thoroughly afterward or your furniture will get "crunchy."

To remove latex paint without heavy chemicals, create a solution of one part dishwashing detergent to twenty parts water. Soak the affected area. Keep rinsing and blotting until it comes clean.

If you spilled wax on your carpet or upholstery, scrape off the excess then set a clean cloth over the wax spot and iron over it using a medium-hot temperature. When you pull off the cloth, the wax will adhere to it. Repeat with fresh sections of the cloth until the wax is gone.

To make a white ring on a polished wood table disappear, rub some real mayonnaise into the mark and let it set for thirty minutes. Buff to polish.

A solution of half vinegar and half water rubbed on with a soft cloth will remove the cloudy buildup of polish on wood surfaces.

To fill light scratches in wood furniture, rub them with a similarly colored crayon until smooth, then wipe away the excess and polish with a standard furniture polish.

Remove smoke stains from fireplace glass with a spray of $1/4$ cup vinegar and 1 tablespoon ammonia in 2 quarts warm water. Wipe with a lint-free cloth.

Order—It's a Good Thing

Organized stuff not only looks better, it's easier to use. Get your kids involved by making organizing video games and DVDs a contest. The winner gets to stay up later to watch his favorite one.

Everyone's family is different, so keep items such as DVDs, CDs, and videos in ways that work for yours. Here are some organizing categories to consider:

Frequency of use Keep your favorites in the front of the storage unit so you can see and retrieve them easily.

Size If you put small things in the front, you

can see what's behind them much more easily. This also creates a calm look—everything is nicely lined up and fairly symmetrical.

■ **Theme** If it's organized by genre, like action and comedy for movies and rock, jazz, and classical for music, you can easily find what you're in the mood to watch or listen to. This order works best if labeled.

■ **Alphabetical order** It's the quickest way to find just what you're looking for, but also the quickest one to go out the window, especially if you have young kids.

What's in Your Toy Box?

If your house is like mine, chances are there's a lot of stuff in the toy box that your kids never use. Cleaning it out may be low on the priority list, but if you don't do it occasionally, you'll find yourself living more in romper room than your family room. So how can you keep control of the toys?

■ **Double their pleasure.** Have two toy boxes—one for big toys and one for small. It's easier for the kids to find the toys with small accessories if they're stored separately.

■ **Give a lesson in charity.** If your kids say they "love" every single toy they have—and much more so when it's time to retire them—change your tack. Suggest they give one toy that has brought them a lot of happiness to a child who might need it.

■ **Make a buck or two.** If you have toys that aren't being used but are in really good condition, photograph the toys and put them up for sale on eBay. Who knows, you may rake in enough to justify buying this year's new holiday "It" toy.

■ **Everything old can be new again.** Retire toys for six months if your kids haven't been playing with them. If they're still not interested when you bring them out of storage, get rid of them (the toys, that is).

■ **Timing is everything.** A really good time to downsize the toy box is right after a birthday or the holidays when your kids are happily distracted by the bright and shiny new things.

Sleep Tight:

Chaos-Free Bedrooms

Bedrooms have become multipurpose rooms— not just where we dress and sleep, but where we watch TV,

PRIORITY LEVEL:
Medium

NEEDS CLEANING:
About once a week

exercise, do chores and paperwork. They're also the spaces where everyone's personal stuff ends up, which makes them not very easy to keep tidy or clean. How can we return them to the meccas of relaxation they are meant to be?

BEDROOMS

A messy, chaotic bedroom is about as far from a sanctuary as you can get. Add to the equation sleep-interrupting allergens that collect in bedding and it's amazing that anyone gets any rest at all. So most of us find it easier to sleep in our bedrooms if we shovel them out occasionally.

In this chapter we'll go over how to make these would-be havens restful as well as hygienic.

Keeping Chaos Under Control

The tasks of weekly bedroom cleaning can be cut dramatically if you stay on top of the clutter. That means—you guessed it—putting things away regularly. Encourage your kids to look after their own spaces and reward good behavior. Here are some ways to keep bedrooms in reasonable shape between weekly cleanings:

In your room

■ Make your bed as soon as you get out of it. If it's as habitual as brushing your teeth, it will be as easy to do.

■ When you dress for work, hang hangers back in the closet and close the door. Put nightwear in the hamper or, folded, under the pillow.

■ Take your morning coffee cup and any glasses from the night before to the kitchen sink.

■ Keep a wastebasket on either side of the bed, lined with plastic bags so you can easily tie up refuse and take it out regularly.

■ Throw old magazines, or newspapers you finished reading the night before, into the recycle bin.

■ Put away the small stuff like jewelry after you wear it so there's less clutter on surfaces.

In your kids' rooms

■ Encourage your kids to put dirty clothes in the hamper and to hang or shelve clothes they'll wear again.

■ Make it a rule that kids over eight take their clothes to the laundry room at least once a week—and

sweaty sports clothes or wet towels, every day.

■ If they're doing their own laundry, tell them they can't take any clothes back to their rooms unless they put them *all* away. (They're not going to want to get dressed in the laundry room every morning.)

■ Try to enforce a house rule of no eating or drinking in bedrooms. Since we know that won't last, at least insist that all dishes, etc., and uneaten food go back to the kitchen before bedtime. (The one exception might be a water glass.)

■ Make sure kids have enough storage to put away their things. In addition to dressers and adequate closet space, you'll want toy and book storage for younger kids, computer-equipment, CD, and book storage for older ones.

■ Store sporting equipment and outdoor-use toys in the garage (see page 156) or a closet.

■ Consider using a number of smaller boxes and bins and spaces for toys rather than one big toy box (or heap). Trains go on this shelf, stuffed animals go in this basket, cars go in this bin, dolls in this one, etc.

■ Attach hooks (at kid height for the young ones) at the side of the closet or along a wall so that frequently used clothing—pajamas, a favorite jacket or sweater—can be easily put away.

BEDROOMS:
5 Minute Attack

You Will Need

**A BOX OR BASKET
(TO COLLECT CLUTTER)
PAPER TOWELS AND DUST CLOTH**

Make the Bed

1 MINUTE

■ Smooth out the sheets and pull them straight. Fluff the pillows.

■ Pull up the blankets.

■ Cover everything with the bedspread, quilt, or duvet and smooth it.

Clear Off the Bureau

1 MINUTE

■ Clear away clutter from the dresser or bureau.

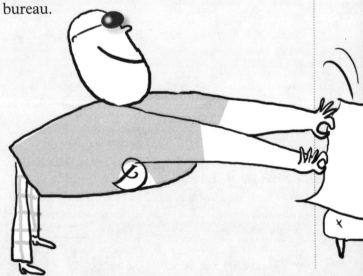

■ Straighten whatever's left on the surface, whether it's hairbrushes and combs or a stack of envelopes.

■ Wipe off surface dust.

Clear the Floor

1 MINUTE

■ In kids' rooms, gather toys and toss them into their designated homes.

■ Empty the wastebasket.

■ Put shoes in the closet.

Put Away Clothes

2 MINUTES

■ Pick up clean clothes—jackets or pants hanging on the back of a chair, for example— and put them away.

■ Gather up any dirty clothes and carry them to the hamper.

■ Tuck pajamas under the pillow.

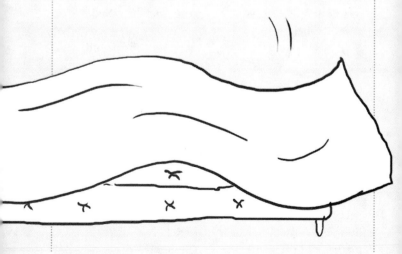

BEDROOMS

Don't Let the Bed Bugs Bite

Bedding traps dust mites, which cause most allergies. One of the best ways to protect your family's bedrooms and sinuses is to buy allergen-resistant dust covers for their mattresses and pillows. These encase a mattress like a zippered bag and are placed under the mattress pad (which can also be hypoallergenic). The pillow covers also zip directly over the pillow and then slip right into the pillowcase.

Bed Making for Beginners

The phrase "looking like an unmade bed" is a byword for sloppiness. So, avoid it. If you make the bed every morning, even a not-so-clean room can often pass for one. Here are some easy-to-master bed-making basics:

■ Once a week, strip the bed and put on fresh sheets. (The mattress pad and blankets should be washed every other month or as needed.) Before you put on a fitted sheet, smooth out the mattress pad and make sure it's secured at the corners.

■ Put the fitted sheet on the farthest, hardest-to-reach corner first, then pull the sheet to an opposite corner, and so on. Smooth out any wrinkles.

■ Unfold the top sheet and center it over the bed, with the wrong side up and the wide hem at the head of the mattress.

■ Put on the blankets, tucking them in at the bottom. Fold the top sheet back over the blankets so that a strip of the right side shows over the top. (This keeps your chin off the blankets and keeps them cleaner longer.) Slide the pillows into their cases, fluff them, and put them at the head of the bed.

■ Lay the top cover (bedspread, quilt, comforter) over the bed. Unless you have pillow shams, pull the spread over the pillows as well, letting it hang down evenly all around.

If you're not changing the sheets, strip the bed down to the fitted sheet and smooth it thoroughly. As you add layers to the bed, give each a good shake.

Flipping the Mattress

In the same way that car experts tell you to drive your factory-new vehicle under 60 mph for the first 1,000 miles and get bimonthly tuneups, mattress companies tell you to flip your mattress once a month for the first six months and four times a year after that. I'm sure this is good advice, but I've never done it and I suspect I'm not alone. Mattresses do need turning, however, for your comfort and for even wear, though maybe not as often as manufacturers suggest. I try to flip at the start of each season on this schedule:

> *Fall:* end to end
> *Winter:* side to side
> *Spring:* end to end
> *Summer:* side to side

To help you remember which way you flipped it last, stick a piece of masking tape on one edge of the mattress and write down the date and direction of the flip. Replace as necessary.

Now Make It Like a Man

I just gave you tips on how to make a traditional bed, but as a guy, I actually don't like a lot of bedclothes and don't have them. In my experience, though, women like traditional, rather complicated beds.

The Girly Way

This kind of elaborate construction is why it's daunting for men to make the bed every morning, and why changing and washing the sheets and rebuilding the layers on the bed, including all those decorative pillows (that are not meant to be slept on), can become a huge production.

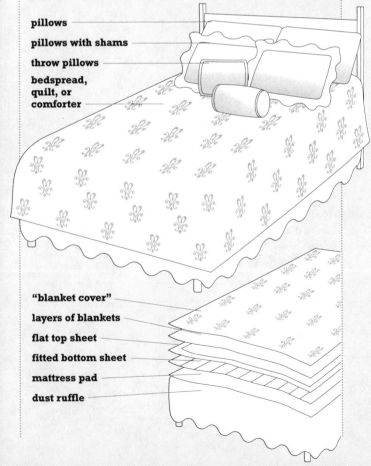

pillows
pillows with shams
throw pillows
bedspread, quilt, or comforter

"blanket cover"
layers of blankets
flat top sheet
fitted bottom sheet
mattress pad
dust ruffle

Dad's Duvet Way

I have another method, and maybe you can coax your wife into doing this, too. I call it the "duvet way." The secret is to use a duvet cover the way that it was intended to be used: as a top sheet, blanket, and cover all in one. Easy to make, easy to wash.

The duvet lifestyle is an easy one. (Worried about how to get the duvet into the cover? See page 124.) Make your bed in the morning by smoothing the duvet over the bottom sheet and straightening the pillows. Plain and simple. There's nothing extra, nothing to tuck in, and it's warm and comfortable. And having a duvet cover that can be removed and washed means you won't have to dry-clean your comforter, because it won't get dirty.

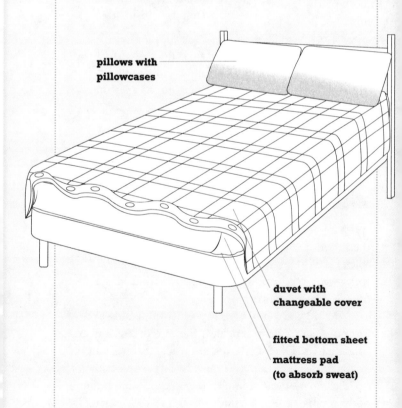

pillows with
pillowcases

duvet with
changeable cover

fitted bottom sheet

mattress pad
(to absorb sweat)

Everyday Duvet

Sometimes people avoid duvets because putting on the cover seems daunting. It isn't. Just follow these simple steps and, with a little practice, it will take you about a minute and a half.

1. Turn the clean duvet cover inside out.

2. Reach both hands into the opening and gather the fabric up your arms until you reach the two top corners of the cover.

3. Holding these two top corners (the stitched-up ones) of fabric, with your arms inside the "bag" of the cover, grasp the two top corners of the duvet itself and shake the cover down over the duvet.

4. Release the top edges and pull the rest of the cover over the duvet to the bottom edges.

5. Grasp the bottom edges of both cover and duvet and shake vigorously. The duvet should spread itself smoothly inside the cover.

6. Button or snap the bottom, and then spread over the bed. You're set for the week!

The Weekly Bedroom Clean

Despite your best efforts to keep on top of the bedroom clutter, you're probably going to have to pick up clothing before your weekly cleaning and put it where it belongs—in the hamper, the closet, or the dresser drawer.

Before you get to the nitty-gritty of dusting and vacuuming the bedroom, clear the tops of dressers and night tables. Take dirty cups to the kitchen, toss out old magazines, and put everything else—books, jewelry, medications—away. To make it easier to vacuum the kids' rooms, take in a laundry basket to collect games, art supplies, toys, and stuff from the floor.

Strip the bed and put the sheets (or duvet cover) in the hamper, but don't make the bed right away. Give the mattress and mattress pad a little time to air out.

BEDROOMS

Vacuum Central

Bedrooms may be the most important places to vacuum in the home, especially if you or your children have allergies or asthma. If you vacuum the bigger reservoirs of dust, like the floor, every week, the smaller ones, like the top of the bedside table, will stay cleaner longer. The brush attachment of your vacuum cleaner can be used around windows and doors; the small upholstery attachment, for the sides of the box spring.

If you have hardwood floors, vacuum them with the bare-floor attachment or setting, then swab with a sponge mop, rinsing the mop every few strokes. (For more about taking care of hardwood floors, see page 109).

Here are the places you don't want to miss when vacuuming:

under beds and furniture	**sides of bed frame and box spring**
corners and tops of wainscoting and skirting boards	**mattress (if not covered with an allergy protector)**
lamp shades and bases	**blinds and louvered doors**
tops of doors and picture frames	**vent covers**
	throw rugs

Keeping Dust at Bay

Dusting the bedroom is as crucial as vacuuming for removing allergens that disturb breathing and, therefore, rest. Dressers, nightstands, armoires, etc., should be done at least once a week with furniture polish and clean microfiber or cotton cloths. Mirrors should also be cleaned weekly. Once a month, vacuum all the books in the bookcase with the dust attachment or a microfiber cloth. Also every month or so, dust air vents, radiators, and heating ducts, as well as blinds, with a vacuum attachment. Lamp shades, lamps, and delicate decorative items can be dusted with a clean paintbrush or feather duster lightly spritzed with Endust.

BEDROOMS

Tips for Cleaning Little Kids' Rooms

Young children need a clean room for their safety. Involve your little one in the job. Ask if he would like you to help him clean rather than asking him to help you.

■ Make sure your younger children have enough storage so they can put away their own toys with ease.

■ Have specific places for bigger toys. Trains on this shelf, big teddy on that. Younger kids like to sort and handle their possessions, so let them.

■ Food in young children's rooms is best avoided. Otherwise, you may be scraping a six-week-old banana from under the bed.

■ Make plenty of bookshelf space available so kids can stack books and also find them easily. Horizontally, spine out, is easier than vertically for little kids.

■ Offer praise rather than criticism. If the floor is clear, don't go behind your child undoing the work and moving items where you think they should go.

Tips for Teenagers' Rooms

Teens need to define their own space. There's no need to let their bedroom become a battleground. If your teen's room is a mess, ignore it as long as certain items come out regularly:

■ Dirty clothes, especially socks, sports clothes, and wet towels, must go to a hamper or the laundry room.

■ Food and dishes must return to the kitchen daily.

■ If laundry is not forthcoming, your teen must do his own.

Then don't think about it any more.

Stow It

Don't be shy about innovative new storage solutions. The carousel racks that spin take up a lot of space, so get the newer flat hanging racks with multiple bars that hold ties in graduated layers.

Vacuum-sealed bags that allow you to suction the air out and compress the package can be great for sweaters or heavy winter quilts. They not only take up less space but also protect fabrics from insects.

One of the best innovations in closet organization is the two-level hanging rack: It lets you hang shirts on one level and pants and skirts below. I also like the tightly sectioned shelving that lets you stack fewer folded items, like sweaters, neatly instead of in teetering towers of wool on one or two high shelves.

Kids' closets can be outfitted with shelves for toys and games; teenagers, with shelves for models, collectibles, etc. You're sure to find an option that suits your family's needs. See pages 128–129 for some ideas.

Better Storage Means Better Sleep

Maybe Oscar Madison can rest in a bedroom with heaps of clothes and paper scattered everywhere, but that's fiction, guys. (And, remember, he was divorced.) In order to rest, rejuvenate, and recharge our batteries, real-life couples need a certain degree of order.

One of the main keys to making your bedroom restful is not to have anything in it that will cause you to worry and lose sleep. Don't take work into the bedroom with you (this includes bills that need to be paid). And, of course, have plenty of storage to tuck everything away. To make your bedroom more sleep-friendly, start by paring down the contents of dressers, closets, and armoires. Toss or give away things that are never worn. Once you've downsized, you can more easily organize the clothing that's left.

In the laundry chapter, I advise you to put whatever you can on a hanger and store it in the closet. I stand by that principle: The less you have in your drawers, the easier it will be to keep them neat and the more likely you'll be to put things away. (Closets are easier to keep organized than drawers, even when they're overstuffed.)

Closing In on Closets

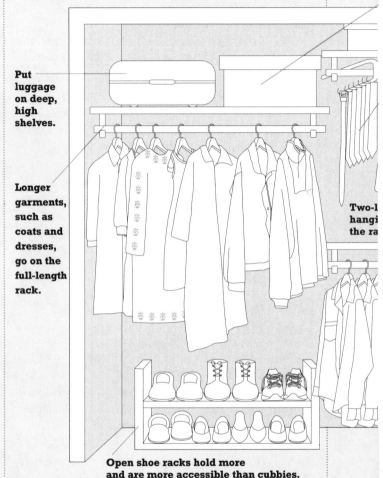

Put luggage on deep, high shelves.

Longer garments, such as coats and dresses, go on the full-length rack.

Two-l hangi the ra

Open shoe racks hold more and are more accessible than cubbies.

One of the best ways to figure out what your closet needs is to open the doors fully and look to see where there's blank space. Is everything crowded on the hanging rack and not reaching to the floor? Are there shelves up high that are holding holiday décor when they should be holding your seasonal clothing? Take a good look at your closet before you look for a closet organizer.

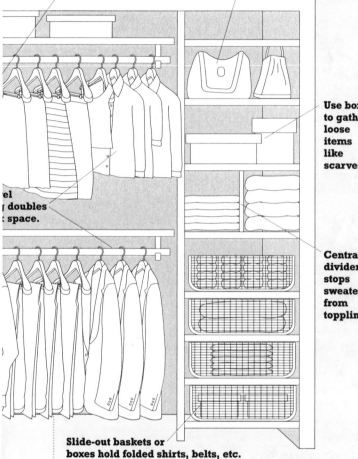

Keep fragile items—crushable hats, delicate sweaters—in boxes.

Flat tie and belt racks take up less space.

Store purses and bags on higher shelves.

Use boxes to gather loose items like scarves.

...el ...g doubles ...space.

Central divider stops sweaters from toppling.

Slide-out baskets or boxes hold folded shirts, belts, etc.

The efficiency and storage that a well-organized closet provides make it worth investing in a closet organizer. You can spend thousands of dollars on closet-organizing systems, but you don't have to. Head to your local home-supply store to find a system that works for you. Remember to measure the dimensions of your closet beforehand, taking into account which way the door hangs and opens, so your system will actually fit!

If you have deep space in your closet, then consider deep drawer units. These can be specially built or you can go with the less expensive option of baskets or storage boxes. Use them on shelves as if they were drawers.

BEDROOMS

The Big Swap: Twice-Yearly Seasonal Storage

To free up more bedroom space, every spring gather and store all cold-weather clothes from your drawers, closets, and shelves, and every autumn, do the opposite. Pick a weekend when the whole family's home and make it a group project.

Clean all clothes before putting them in storage. You'll better ward off insects and vermin that way. Pack nonseasonal clothes in plastic storage bins and stow them in the attic or garage (see Dad's Domain, page 149, for more on this). As you'll see when you start packing things away, it will inspire you to get rid of clothes you no longer wear.

Tips for Expanding Bedroom Storage

N o one says you have to put clothes away in closets or drawers—they just need to be put away. Consider these alternatives to traditional bedroom storage:

■ Shelve one of the walls in the room for storing folded sweaters and jeans.

■ Use a wicker laundry basket for sock and underwear storage.

■ Hang hooks across one wall and arrange easy-on-the eye items like hats, jewelry, scarves, and handbags on them.

■ If there's space for more furniture, bring in an armoire or freestanding wardrobe.

■ In kids' rooms, outfit bookshelves with colorful plastic containers of all sizes to store smaller toys and art supplies. (This solution also works in adults' rooms—just use more sophisticated containers, like wicker or canvas baskets.)

■ Employ under-the-bed storage containers whenever possible.

A Working Retreat:

Home Office Management

Whether you're a bring-work-home Dad, a work-at-home Dad, or a housekeeping Dad who needs a special space to deal with

PRIORITY LEVEL:
Low

NEEDS ATTENTION:
Once a month
(with weekly touchups)

household paperwork, like paying bills and signing report cards—or even a retreat for playing video games or surfing the Net—your home office space needs to be functional and comfortable without being an eyesore to you or the rest of the family. How and why and how often you use your office determines how much household real estate can be devoted to it—from an entire room to a desk tucked away in a bedroom, kitchen, or another room.

In this chapter we'll look at how to set up a home office the Dad way, no matter how little space you have to devote to it, and how to keep it running and organized—and at least "neat enough."

Location Counts

Once upon a time our home office was an actual room, but now that space is more popularly known as the "baby's room." We briefly considered relocating the office to our bedroom, but besides being unable to keep an eye on the kids from that isolated location, working where we would sleep meant we couldn't relax at night. So we agreed on a corner of the living room, where the person at the desk could also watch over the kids.

If you don't yet have a place for your "home office," scout around. Pick about three or four possibilities, then narrow it down. Visualize yourself working in these areas. What are some of the plus sides: a quiet location? a window? an outlet to plug in your computer, lamp, and other electrical devices? And downsides: too cramped? too much traffic passing through?

No matter what you do in your home office, make sure it can be made permanent, even if the space is only big enough for a desk or computer table with a filing system underneath. Having a desktop computer will usually ground you to one spot, but if you're the freewheeling, work-where-you-land laptop type, you still want to have a station where you can work and store important household paperwork. I may not have all my crucial stuff in a watertight box, ready to be grabbed in an emergency (though I swear that's next on my agenda—see page 144), but I know where all those papers are located.

Functional Furnishings

Once you know where your work space will be, it's time to outfit it, starting with the big picture.

Work Surface

A desk with some storage is best (mine is an Ikea job that cost less than $200 and has never given me a moment's difficulty), but a table can also serve your purpose. If you aren't going to be working at a computer desk, choose a table about 29 inches in height. Your arms will get tired if you work at too high a surface, and your neck and back will start giving you trouble if you hunch over a low one.

Keep your work surface as clear as possible; ideally the only things that should be on it when you're not working are a lamp (if needed) and a canister for pens and pencils. (See page 134 for storing other supplies.)

Chair

If you're setting up in a "shared" space—a bedroom, a corner of the kitchen—you may already have a chair in that room, but it probably wasn't designed for poring over paperwork or working at a computer. My advice: Purchase the best desk chair you can afford. You want one with adjustable height that provides good lumbar support. Casters are a good idea, so you can roll back and forth between surfaces, and most office chairs are made with them. (Keep a plastic mat under the chair if you're worried about your floor or carpeting.) Other options depend on your comfort needs—arms, a foot rest, reclining back. Work in the chair for an hour or two and see if you're still comfortable after that time. If not, return it and try another one. My favorite desk chair is a large, inflatable exercise ball. It doesn't hurt my back and I can work on my abs while I pay bills.

Lighting

If you work mostly at a computer, be sure the lighting you choose isn't too bright or you'll have to deal with glare. An ambient light source, such as the overhead lighting that already exists, or a halogen lamp for indirect light should be sufficient.

Drowning in a Sea of Paper? Learn to Swim

Once you have a place for paperwork to collect, like a desktop, you'll think that your junk mail and bills are starting to reproduce overnight. Don't let your new home office become a way station for paper. Put a firm stop to these shenanigans with specific filing and storage systems and a merciless approach to sorting and handling.

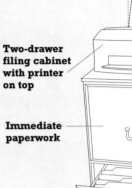

Two-drawer filing cabinet with printer on top

Immediate paperwork

Less recent paperwork

Filing/Storage System

In my home office, I installed shelving above my work space, plus a filing cabinet for current paperwork; the top serves as the printer station. (Long-term paperwork such as your old tax returns don't need to be kept in your office; pack them away in an airtight box in your attic or basement—if it's dry enough.) Here are some things you *will* want to store in your office:

■ Immediate paperwork, such as bills that need to be paid and recent papers that need to be filed, belongs in a standing file on your desk or in the top drawer of your filing cabinet, labeled "To Be Dealt With" and "To Be Filed." (This may sound like an extra step, but it will save time in the long run because if you file when you're actually in the mood, you're less likely to misfile important papers.)

■ Less recent paperwork that may be needed at a moment's notice, such as insurance information or bank statements, should be filed in the bottom drawer.

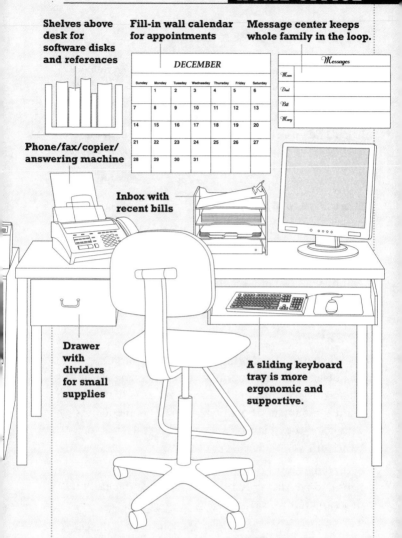

Shelves above desk for software disks and references

Fill-in wall calendar for appointments

Message center keeps whole family in the loop.

DECEMBER						
Sunday	Monday	Tuesday	Wednesday	Thursday	Friday	Saturday
	1	2	3	4	5	6
7	8	9	10	11	12	13
14	15	16	17	18	19	20
21	22	23	24	25	26	27
28	29	30	31			

Messages	
Mom	
Dad	
Bill	
Mary	

Phone/fax/copier/answering machine

Inbox with recent bills

Drawer with dividers for small supplies

A sliding keyboard tray is more ergonomic and supportive.

■ Manuals for your electronic equipment, as well as software disks, can be stored on a shelf or in a nearby cabinet.

■ Only you can decide if In and Out boxes, flat filing trays, or accordion files work on your desktop. Some people keep things moving along from these receptacles; others get hopelessly bogged down.

Other suggestions:

■ Use a hanging clipboard to keep urgent things in the forefront of your mind.

■ Wood or wicker basket drawers are good for storage.

Check out www.aboutstuff.com for more office solutions.

HOME OFFICE

Spaghetti Junction

There's nothing more confusing or unsettling to look at than a writhing mass of power cords that connect to who knows what. A cord organizer keeps all kinds of cords snuggly wrapped together in one neat tube. If you'd rather not spend the money, pull together the spaghetti junction behind your desk and fasten at several points with twist ties.

Electronic Equipment

How much or how little each individual Dad has is up to him. The necessities include a computer with keyboard, mouse, and monitor, as well as a printer. You may also want a scanner, separate photo printer, small copy machine, speakers, and so on.

Supplies

A certain amount of office gear is useful, but don't go nuts at the office-supply store, envisioning all the organizing you're going to do as soon as you lug home a mountain of plastic boxes and 50 file folders with color-coded labels. You won't use it! Here's the basic stuff you do need:

■ A ready supply of pens and pencils, stored in a cup on the desk or in the top drawer

■ Notepads and Post-its, so you can scribble down messages or put reminders to yourself on your computer monitor: "Return library books." "Pay car insurance." "Remember to tell wife that my parents are coming for the weekend!"

■ A wall or desk calendar with family appointments noted; keep it here or on the fridge or wherever you're most likely to write in it and consult it

■ Safety envelopes (the kind you can't see through, for mailing checks) and a good supply of first-class stamps

■ Manila folders and hanging files with tabs for a file drawer

■ Miscellaneous necessities: tape, stapler and staples, rubber bands, paper clips, scissors, letter opener, glue, and other small office supplies

Go Postal on Incoming Mail

Mail is one of the biggest sources of household clutter. With the countless magazines, catalogs, and solicitations that arrive daily, it's no wonder you haven't seen the top of your work surface in months. The best way to avoid the buildup is to take control of this paper storm as it comes in. You might think you don't have time to sort mail daily, but taking a few minutes out of every day will save you an hour or more on the weekend.

Think of your mail in three categories, and deal with it accordingly as soon as you get it.

Throw it away without opening it: Unsolicited offers, catalogs from stores you never heard of and have no interest in, anything that says you won a prize. Toss it in your recycling bin or run the loose papers through the paper shredder (see page 140).

Open it and then throw it away: Unsolicited offers that may sound interesting, like interest-free credit, or a catalog from a place you never heard of but want to check out.

Open it and deal with it: Your most important category, it includes bills that need to be paid, invitations that need replies, and magazines and catalogs you actually ordered.

■ Keep a paper-recycling container in your office. Take the mail immediately to your office and make instant decisions. Recycle magazines and catalogs that won't be read and destroy all loose paper that contains your personal information.

■ Take bills out of their envelopes and nestle them in the flap of the return envelope, if one is included. If you pay bills online, then discard the envelope. Arrange them from soonest due to latest and put in two file folders labeled "Bills Due 1–15" and "Bills Due 16–31." It will speed up the bill-paying process. Ditto for anything else that requires your attention, such as forms to fill out or invitations. File these with the bills, according to due dates.

HOME OFFICE

Home Central

If you're in charge of your household, you know how hard it can be to keep up with everyone's schedules, not to mention paying bills and being on top of all that random stuff, like appointments, invitations, remembering relatives' birthdays, etc. Make your home office your management headquarters and filter all household matters through it. Here are some tips to keep your headquarters organized and functional:

- Hanging pocket files are a great way to keep time-sensitive papers in a highly visible place. Install hooks on the wall or the door in your home office, and hang pockets labeled with the contents—bills, invitations, school notices, tax forms, etc.

- Hang a large wall calendar (with grid space for writing) and assign each family member a different-color pen or marker. (Use black for things that pertain to the entire household.) When an activity or event comes up, write it in on the calendar in the appropriate color. Each day, you'll see at a glance who has to be where and when.

© Sandra Boynton

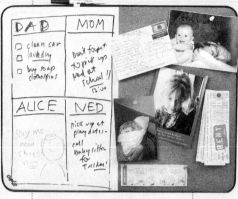

pen and paper handy to take phone messages and to write down anything on the incoming voicemail when you play the messages.

■ Set up biweekly bill-paying sessions with your wife and deal with them together. It might not be the "quality time" you'd like, but it's the

■ Hectic schedules mean family members don't get to (or forget to) tell each other things, so a central location for messages can aid communication. Hang a white board in your home office and separate it into sections labeled for each family member. Have family members write messages to each other with dry-erase markers.

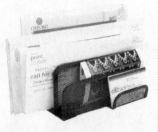

best way to keep you both aware of the finances.

■ Keep a central list here of names, addresses, and phone numbers of grandparents and relatives, schools and teachers, doctors, babysitters, sports teams, playmates' parents, and anyone else your family may need to contact. In an emergency, vital information won't be solely in one person's address book or PDA.

■ Not getting phone messages? Set up a message log right by your phone's answering machine (use a spiral notebook and a pen attached with a rubber band or string). That way there will always be

HOME OFFICE

Boy Toy: Destroying the Evidence

While there are varying levels of sophistication, a paper shredder is essentially a pair of rotating cutting blades, a paper comber, and a motor that drives them. It's used to protect your privacy by shredding all your personal information into illegible bits before putting it back into the world. Just be sure that before you feed any paper to your shredder, you remove all staples, paper clips, rubber bands, or other fasteners.

Bill Paying 101

In an ideal world, you have the cash flow and the inclination to pay your bills as soon as they come in. But if you're like most of us, set a biweekly time for dealing with your bills. Actually, if you want to pay all your monthly bills at one time, most creditors will adjust their due dates to accommodate you. Just pick up the phone and ask.

A great way to eliminate paper coming into your house is to pay bills online and request that your creditors send you e-mail reminders instead of paper statements. You can pay bills through your bank's online service. (Sometimes there's a fee involved.) Aside from no longer having endless paper trails, you also eliminate postage and trips to the mailbox. You can also set up a recurring payment with your bank account so you never have to worry about physically paying a bill—just be sure you note when the money is scheduled to come out of your account *and* that you can cover it.

Internet Safety

It is safest and always preferable to use your bank's online payment system rather than the payment systems of individual billers. The payment systems of banks have the top level of security so you can feel confident that you aren't spreading your personal information throughout the Internet. Plus, it's more efficient—you log on to only one place to pay bills.

Keep It or Toss It?

My dad worked for an insurance company for nearly 40 years, and one of the fatherly bits of experience he passed along was this: Do *not* keep papers that you don't need. Following is a basic guide to what you should keep and roughly how long.

Keep always

- Marriage, birth, and death certificates

- Wills and living wills (to be replaced if updated)

- Social Security cards

- Divorce and settlement documents

- Custody or adoption papers

- Naturalization papers; proof of citizenship if you became a citizen but don't have a passport

- Diplomas and military documents

- Tax returns

Keep for a limited time

- Supporting documentation for tax returns, including receipts and credit card statements— for seven years after return was filed

- Stocks, bonds, securities, savings certificates, bank account info, bank statements—for duration of ownership, and then seven more years in case needed for tax purposes

- Cancelled checks— for three years

- Car registration and insurance cards—only the current versions

- Passports—until renewed (every 10 years)

Cyber-Manuals

When you buy a new appliance or electronic item today, most likely the manual will be online. Do an online search for the exact name of the item, such as "Super DVD Player CJ-234 manual." It will likely be available as a pdf file. Download it and keep it in a manual folder on your computer (and back it up as you would all your files). This way, you can discard the paper "Manuals" and cut down a bit more on clutter.

HOME OFFICE:

5 Minute Attack

You Will Need

RECYCLING CONTAINER
PAPER TOWELS
FURNITURE POLISH
GLASS CLEANER
BROOM AND/OR VACUUM CLEANER
CAN OF FORCED AIR
MICROFIBER CLOTH OR COTTON RAG
PAPER SHREDDER (OPTIONAL)

Sort Through the Paper

2 MINUTES

■ Open the mail. Toss out junk mail without opening it (shred unwanted credit card offers or anything that can be used fraudulently if found in the trash). Put catalogs and magazines you want to read in one stack (those you don't in recycling); put open bills in another.

■ Put loose papers in your "To Be Filed" folder for when you have more time to deal with them.

Tidy the Desktop

1 MINUTE

■ Straighten any remaining papers.

■ Spray glass cleaner or furniture polish, depending on your work surface, and wipe desk clean with a paper towel.

■ Tuck office supplies in desk drawers.

Finishing Touches

2 MINUTES

■ Sweep or vacuum the area around your work space (all that paper generates a lot of dust).

■ Take the can of forced air and blow dust and debris out of the cracks between the keyboard keys.

■ Dust off the computer monitor and wipe the mouse.

HOME OFFICE

■ Warranties and manuals for electronics and appliances—for the duration of ownership. Keep all the manuals related to office equipment in a file in the office, with receipts or original bills of sale stapled to the front. (Manuals for other household equipment can be kept in the kitchen; see page 23.)

The Crucial Stuff: Building an Emergency File

If, heaven forbid, you have to rebuild your life from nothing, it's going to be a lot easier if you have a packet containing the following information and documents, or copies of them, to grab in an emergency.

■ Credit-card account numbers, names of all family members who hold a copy of the card, and toll-free numbers for the issuers

■ Insurance policy numbers and contact number for insurer

■ Health-insurance policy numbers and contact info

■ Social Security and passport numbers for all family members

■ All bank-account numbers, PINs, toll-free contact numbers, and ID and password for online banking

■ Other savings or investment accounts, toll-free contact numbers, and PINs or passwords

■ Serial numbers or other identifying numbers for stocks or bonds and contact info for issuers

■ Copies of wills and living wills

■ Copies of powers of attorney

■ Copies of deeds (house, cars, boat, etc.)

■ Copies of major insurance policies (car, house, rental property, etc.)

■ Copies of major employee benefits

■ Health, car, life insurance info

■ Inventory list or digital photo files of important household items (jewelry, cameras, electronics, etc.)

■ Copies of passports

If you're worried about having this info only on paper, store it in an encrypted file on a disk, sending copies to a trusted friend or relative.

The Home Office Clean

Even if you're not in your home office that often, dust happens. Here's what you need to do every other week or so in addition to the 5-Minute Attack:

■ Completely clear away the paperwork on your desk. Go into your files, and put those papers in the folders where they belong.

■ With glass cleaner or furniture polish and a clean paper towel, wipe down not only the top of your desk but also the sides and back legs. Dust your desk chair.

■ Spritz all-purpose cleaner onto a paper towel and wipe the phone (base and handset) and desk lamp. Wipe down other equipment, but not your computer. (See the special techniques for this below.)

■ Empty your paper shredder or recycling container right into a plastic paper-recycling bag and put it outside with the rest of the refuse.

■ Vacuum or mop the area.

Cleaning Your Computer

Computers get surprisingly dirty, especially since, despite manufacturers' warnings, we often eat while using them. But keep in mind, computers aren't like cars: They can't take a lot of buffing and polishing, so you only want to clean your computer once a month or even every couple of months.

Here are some tips for keeping it clean:

■ Always turn off the computer and unplug it before cleaning.

■ It's safest to clean a flat screen with a lens cloth and lens cleaner or with a premoistened lens towelette. Handle the surface gently when cleaning (too much pressure can damage the screen).

■ If you have an older CRT monitor (the kind with a tube, like a TV screen), wipe it with a soft lint-free cloth lightly dampened with a glass cleaner. Don't spray glass cleaner directly at

the monitor and don't joggle it around too much when cleaning.

■ With a soft, lint-free cloth lightly dampened with water, wipe down the exterior case. It is better not to use an all-purpose spray cleaner, as you don't want chemicals near your vents. (If you must use an all-purpose cleaner, be sure to spray it on the cloth and not on the computer.)

■ Clean an optical mouse with a damp cloth. Take special care around the laser part. For a track ball mouse, follow manufacturer's instructions to take apart the mechanism and wipe it, usually with rubbing alcohol.

■ Spray a can of forced air between the crevices of the keyboard to remove debris. You can also use a clean paintbrush to lightly and briskly brush along the rows, getting between the keys as gently as you can, then use the vacuum nozzle to suck up the dust you've loosened.

■ Grease deposits from your fingers may make keyboards especially dirty over time. I still prefer to wipe the keys with water, but if you use a cleaner, such as a window spray or rubbing alcohol, always

What's Inside Also Counts!

Wiping the exterior of your computer is only half the battle. If your computer files are a mess, you won't be able to work efficiently. You might want to do this cleanup monthly or twice a year. Here are some tips for getting those files in order.

■ Before you delete files strewn all over your messy desktop, back up everything on CDs or DVDs (the latter hold a lot more) or even onto a spare hard drive.

■ Sort all the scattered documents into named folders. Go to the pull-down menu marked "File" and click on "New" and then "Folder." You can make as many new folders and subfolders as you like. Folders can contain files from different programs. So you might have a file marked "This Year's Taxes," which can hold Word documents, spreadsheets, and jpeg scans of your credit-card documents (if you're that organized).

■ If you share the home computer, you may want to make a folder for each of you and store your own folders inside.

■ If you have dozens, or hundreds, of old documents cluttering your system and you're sure you don't need them anymore, delete them. I keep one folder of "Old Stuff" for anything I think I *might* need (and yet never do) and delete the rest.

■ Keep your e-mail inbox as empty as possible. It's like opening mail. Don't let stuff just sit there. Deal with it: Save it in a subfolder if you need it and trash it if you don't.

■ Install a good spam filter and *use it.* Your ISP may have one on offer, or your e-mail program may have a good one in place. Most modern spam filters are set to "learn" what's spam and what's not by having you mark things as "junk" when they come in or, occasionally, "This is not junk," when you find an old friend's e-mail sitting in the junk file.

■ Keep an up-to-date virus scanner on your computer and run it regularly. There are lots of commercial scanners available and even some free utilities that you can search for on the Web and download.

put it on the cloth, not on the keyboard. Use a soft, clean, lint-free cloth and rub each key gently until clean.

■ Let the computer sit for at least an hour or so to be sure that everything is totally dry before plugging it back in.

■ As an annual or semiannual task, lightly vacuum over the vents on the back of the computer with the small brush attachment. Dust can block the air vents and internal fans inside that keep your motherboard from overheating. Brush gently over the surface; you don't want to force dust *into* the vents.

Dad's Domain:

Attics, Basements, and Garages

I don't go into my attic that often, but if I didn't have it, it would be hard to live in the other two floors of my house: I use the attic to store all the stuff that would be in the way

PRIORITY LEVEL:
Low to Medium

NEEDS CLEANING:
Seasonally
(can sometimes be put off to once a year)

elsewhere. Basements and garages can serve the same purpose, but they also offer more opportunities for usable space on a regular basis: a Dad-centric workshop to keep your tools readily at hand or a family "locker room" that makes sports equipment easy to grab.

Even if you don't have a "finished" basement or a storage-ready attic, you can prep these spaces pretty easily to provide storage. This chapter will show you how to make these areas dry, odor- and vermin-free, insulated, and ventilated for maximum usefulness.

Dad's Plan of Attack

To get started, you may need to empty these spaces. (Do one per day or you'll end up with stuff all over your house and lawn.) As you're cleaning stuff out, decide what you need to schlep back and what you can do without. Not sure what to keep and what to toss?

What stays:

- holiday decorations
- mementos
- important non-current paperwork
- unexpired surplus foods and dry goods
- off-season clothing
- sporting goods
- tools
- paint, chemicals, etc.

What goes:

- broken toys
- ratty or outmoded clothes
- clothes that no longer fit
- worn-out books
- rusty tools
- anything that's been sitting there with no purpose for more than a year— you get the idea

Stuff that's not useful to you anymore but still in fairly good condition can be loaded into the back of your car and taken to a local charity. The other stuff goes to the dump. Better yet, try to time your clean-out when your town is doing a big curbside pickup. Once you've cleaned out each of these spaces, it's time to prep it to maximize its storage potential.

Preparing Your Attic for Storage

Older houses were generally built with the expectation that the attic would be used for storage and even an extra sleeping space, but newer homes (built in the last 20 to 30 years) often have engineered roof trusses and narrow joists that weren't designed to bear weight. So double-check that the attic can bear the weight long-term:

■ Measure the width of the joists, the distance between them (measure from the start of one joist to the start of the next), and the distance between the walls that support them. Take this information to a lumberyard. They have span charts that will tell you what weight your floor can support and what kind of reinforcements (such as "sister joists") you might need to add.

■ If your joists are strong enough, lay a plywood floor as a support for boxes or low shelves.

■ Additional insulation may be necessary for long-term storage, to control both temperature and moisture. Discuss the efficiency of your attic insulation (the R value, or thermal resistance to heat flow) with your local home-repair store to find out the optimal insulation for your climate.

■ Control ventilation with an extractor and ventilator fan. Ideally, it should have a thermostat that kicks on the fan when the temperature reaches a certain point as well as a safety shutoff for excessively high temperatures (to stop the fan from fueling a fire in floors below). It should also have a humidity sensor that triggers the fan when the humidity increases.

DAD *to* **DAD**

If you use mothballs when you store clothes, tuck them away in places that children won't find them—perhaps in a mesh bag hidden inside the garment bag or box. This will keep curious children safe as well as contain the odor.

Storing Clothes Off-Season

As we saw in the bedroom chapter, most of us can't fit the contents of a year-round wardrobe into the bedroom. Here are some tips to keep items fresh, insect-free, and ready to wear when the seasons change:

■ Launder or dry-clean all clothes before storing them.

■ Avoid storing clothes in excessively humid spaces (this is why dry attics make better storage areas than basements do).

■ Keep stored clothing away from light, which will cause fading.

■ Store cotton, wool, silk, and linen in well-ventilated areas in non-airtight containers such as a hanging garment bag. These materials need to "breathe."

■ When you take clothes out of storage, toss them in the dryer on low with a dryer sheet for about 10 minutes to freshen them up and get rid of wrinkles.

Preparing Your Basement for Storage

Finished or not, basements collect moisture. Because they are located mostly below ground, the coolness of the earth against the walls draws condensation and concentrates it here. For that reason, avoid storing items below ground that can be damaged by mold and mildew, such as books and clothing. Here are some ways to keep your basement dry:

■ Run a dehumidifier. If you have serious dampness problems, buy an energy-efficient model that can run continuously (or one with a timer that runs it half the time). It's smart to get one with a self-draining unit that can run directly into your floor drain or into a hose and out the window. That way you won't have to remember to empty the collector pan.

■ Insulate really humid basements above the frost line by screwing studs to the walls and adding insulation between them. (Ask at your local hardware store for the appropriate R value of insulation and also where to find the frost line in your region.)

■ Exposed stone, brick, or cement foundation walls can be painted with a masonry sealer, finished walls with a moisture-blocking paint. Again, consult your friendly hardware-store guys.

■ Discard previously stored items that already show signs of mold or mildew damage. Spray a commercial mildew killer on the walls and floor, or if it's impossible to keep kids and animals away from the area, try Dad's Own Mildew Remover, page 154.

■ Sweep and mop the floor, using a wet-dry vac if you have one, and allow it to dry thoroughly before putting anything back.

When the Basement Is Also the Laundry Room

In many houses basements are home to washing machine and dryer, ironing board and iron, and everything else to do with the laundry. Here are some tips for keeping the cleaning area clean:

■ Store all laundry supplies on an eye-level shelf on the wall behind the washer or in a rolling caddy. Keep a roll of paper towels and an all-purpose spray cleaner here, as well, and wipe down the machines when necessary.

■ Place an empty coffee can or plastic dish by the washer for the forgotten contents of pockets, like lipsticks, pens, crayons, and other laundry menaces. Also keep a trash can by the washer for lint and pocket contents and for cleaning the lint filter on the dryer.

■ If you have the room, establish a presort system.

Label five separate bins and encourage family members to take their clothes to the laundry room and place them in the appropriate bins: whites, colors and darks, linens, hand-washables and gentles, and dry cleaning.

■ Keep a folding drying rack in the laundry room to hang clothes that don't go in the dryer. Invest in a portable hanging rod and keep empty hangers on hand.

■ Don't take lone socks out of the laundry room. If you set up a spot to keep them, their prodigal partners do eventually turn up.

Dad's Own Mildew Remover

Again, I'm not a fan of strong chemicals, so I'm always looking for ways to improve on them. Here are two solutions for eradicating mildew, one regular and one extra strength.

Regular strength
> **1 cup white vinegar**
> **1 cup dishwashing liquid**
> **$1/2$ cup salt**

Wearing rubber gloves, mix the ingredients in a basin. Soak a heavy-duty sponge or brush in the solution, then scrub away the mildew patches. Allow the cleaner to stand for 2 to 3 hours. Then rinse well.

Extra strength
> **2 cups warm water**
> **$1/4$ cup white vinegar**
> **1 tablespoon borax**

Mix in a clean spray bottle, spray liberally over mildew-prone areas, and allow to dry. Repeat every 3 to 4 weeks until your mildew problem is under control.

The Rules of Play: Sporting Goods at Your Fingertips

Your best bet is to keep sporting goods in the garage, where they are easily accessible when it's time to head out and play. Here are some tips to keep sports storage under control:

■ Store balls in plastic bins, separated by size—basketballs, volleyballs, and footballs in one container, softballs, baseballs, and tennis balls in another, racquetballs and golf balls in yet another.

■ On one wall install a pegboard with ¼-inch holes (that size can hold the most weight). Hang hockey and lacrosse sticks from hooks in the board, as well as skateboards, ice skates, air pumps, and even bicycles and helmets.

■ Assign a different-color storage bin to each family member for miscellaneous equipment, like catcher's mitts and cleats.

■ Store baseball bats and other long, narrow pieces of sports equipment (including hockey and lacrosse sticks) in a barrel or garbage can that's at least three-fourths the height of the tallest stick.

Garage-A-Go-Go

Because the garage is generally above ground, it tends to stay dryer than the basement, well ventilated, and sometimes partially heated if it's connected to the house. This makes garages great for storage, not to mention a good spot for Dad's workshop or tool bench, as well as a place for sports and garden equipment.

Getting safely to and from your car should be your first priority, so make sure there's a clear path from the garage door to the front wall and to any other door or exit. Then you can make room for storage.

If you don't keep a car here, remove all traces of former occupancy by cars. If there are oil stains on the floor, sprinkle them thickly with a mixture of baking soda and cornmeal, leave it overnight, then sweep it up with a broom and dustpan. Get rid of any remaining stain by wetting the area and scrubbing with generous amounts of baking soda and a stiff work brush.

DAD *to* DAD

Keep your gutters clean and make sure they empty at least a yard from your exterior walls. If they don't, purchase drain extenders, which fit onto the bottom of a downpipe and can be slanted to carry the water away from your basement.

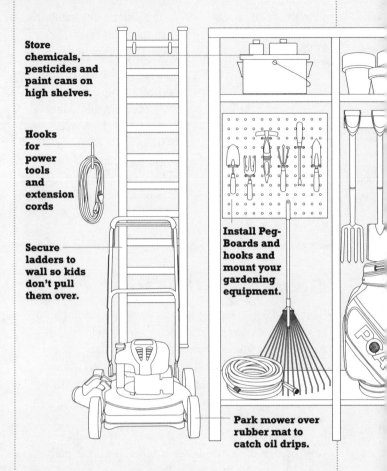

Store chemicals, pesticides and paint cans on high shelves.

Hooks for power tools and extension cords

Secure ladders to wall so kids don't pull them over.

Install Peg-Boards and hooks and mount your gardening equipment.

Park mower over rubber mat to catch oil drips.

How Does Your Garage (Equipment) Grow?

A modular metal storage rack is ideal for storing garage equipment, and you can add as many units as you need.

■ Keep garden tools off the ground, both to prevent rust and to keep them high and safe from little hands.

■ Put chemicals and pesticides on the highest shelves. If there's any risk of your child

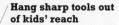

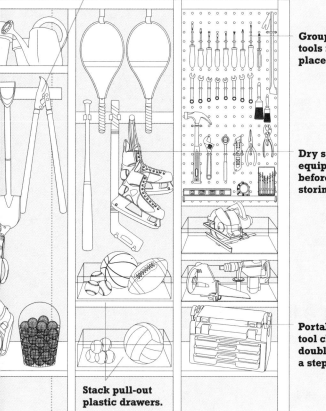

Hang sharp tools out of kids' reach

Group like tools in one place.

Dry sports equipment before storing.

Portable tool chest doubles as a step stool.

Stack pull-out plastic drawers.

climbing, store them in locked boxes.

■ Clean soil off garden tools to prevent rust.

■ Clean sweat and dirt from sports equipment before storing.

■ Dispose of used rags and keep clean rags in a dry space away from combustibles like solvents.

■ Store paint cans on a shelf, not on the floor, to prevent dampness from rusting the base.

■ Clean lawn mowers before bringing them inside for the winter. Now is a good time to change the oil and sharpen the blade each year. Ideally, drain the gas out before storing.

■ Drain garden hoses and coil them loosely before bringing inside for the winter so they don't freeze and crack in the cold weather.

DAD'S DOMAIN

Racking It Up

Now that you've prepped your attic, basement, and garage, you need to devise a plan for where to actually put all your stuff. Here are some suggestions:

■ **Invest in modular metal or plastic shelving** —it's worth the expense, especially in basements, where it can protect items from flooding or dampness through the floor. (Wooden shelving is far more likely to buckle or succumb to water damage.)

■ **Attach modular shelving to a wall for stability.** Don't skip this instruction even if the shelves look solid without wall support— a curious, climbing child could topple the unit.

■ **Don't store current or important papers** in these spaces. Crucial

Dad's Own Bug Killer

The proximity of your house, with its warmth and food supplies, may attract vermin such as roaches and silverfish to the garage. Make an insect killer that's safe for children and pets by mixing 2 parts baking soda with 1 part sugar. Sprinkle along the walls.

The Workshop: A Man's Private Space

If you have any room left with the car and other items in there, the garage is a great place to set up a workshop. Like any other space in the home, however, you don't want it to become chaos central. Here are some tips for setting up your garage or basement workshop:

■ Even if you have ample space, minimize the room you take up. Build a fold-up workbench that you can fold down only when you need it. The average six-foot guy can work with ease at a bench 34 to 36 inches high; if you're taller or shorter than average, adjust the height so it's comfortable for you.

■ Install a Peg-Board and hooks on at least one wall and hang your tools. Group like tools—all screwdrivers in one place, etc.

■ If your garage is damp, store metal tools in sealed wooden bins filled with camphor and sawdust to prevent rusting.

■ Invest in a plastic storage system that separates nails and screws by category and store it under your workbench. You can also sort them into glass jars on a shelf. (For under-shelf storage, nail the lids to the bottom of the shelf, then twist the jars onto the lids.)

■ Wind and tie up all cords for power tools before hanging them. Install a hook over your workbench to hold the slack while you're using them.

■ Keep a cordless drill recharging here for household tasks. It's a crucial home repair tool that can double as an electric screwdriver.

■ This is the place to store extension cords so you can always find them, from 6-foot indoor ones to a 50-foot outdoor cord.

■ Never clean your metal tools with water. If you need to clean tools, spray the surface with WD-40 and scrub off any rust or debris with a plastic scrubbing pad. Wipe clean with a soft, absorbent cloth.

■ Make saw blades and table-saw beds glide smoothly by rubbing a little paste wax onto the surface. Dry for 20 minutes, then buff with a soft, dry cloth.

DAD'S DOMAIN

Where Do I Put That?

The best thing about having an attic, basement, or garage—or all three—is that you can store stuff here that you need once in a while but can't possibly live with. So much doesn't belong in the main areas of your home, it's almost impossible for me to list what you can store in these spaces. Here's a quick-reference storage checklist for common extracurricular household items.

Items to store	How to store	Where to store
Holiday decorations	In airtight plastic bins, labeled with the holiday and contents	Attic
Folding chairs	Covered with a tarp or old bed sheet	Attic or basement
Out-of-season clothes	In plastic bins—not airtight—or hung in large garment bags	Attic
Mementos	In plastic bins or archival photo shoe boxes, sorted by year and name of owner	Attic
Surplus canned and dried foods	In airtight containers	Basement
Gardening tools and equipment	On a Peg-Board or a shelving system (see page 156)	Garage

documents like marriage or adoption certificates should be stored in your home office area (see page 141).

■ **Avoid using cardboard boxes.** While these are handy and economical, they are porous and defenseless against moisture, temperature swings, and moths. Opt instead for plastic storage bins— airtight ones for papers, ventilated ones for clothing.

■ **Use a pallet on a cellar floor** when storing furniture, even if the floor is finished. (For extra protection, I'd cover the pallet with plastic sheeting and then place the furniture on top

Items to store	How to store	Where to store
Luggage	In closed plastic garbage bags or on a wall-mounted luggage rack	Attic
Paint/chemicals	On a high shelf out of reach of children	Garage, or basement if your garage goes below freezing
Spare batteries, lightbulbs	On a shelf near the door for easy access	Basement
Lawn furniture	Under a sheet or tarp	Garage or basement
Tax documents from previous years and other financial paperwork that needs to be kept	In airtight plastic bins or banker's boxes, labeled with the year and nature of the documents	Attic
Ratty old sweater from high school	In a large garbage bag with like items	Garbage
Rusty tricycle your kids outgrew more than five years ago	Pull it to the curb on garbage pick-up day	Garbage

before covering it with a tarp or dust sheet.)

■ **Don't stack boxes on furniture.** Eventually the weight will weaken the furniture joints and will crush upholstery and cushions.

■ **Nail basic wood frames** in spaces with exposed rafters or joists. These can be vertical 2 × 4s) with a 2 × 4 or plywood "base" to hold sports equipment such as skis and sleds or workshop supplies such as lumber, or gutters and pipes.

■ **Make a wine cellar.** If your cellar seems much too damp to store anything in, you can always turn it into a wine cellar. Wines are happiest stored on their sides in a damp place at around 50°F, which allows them to age better and keeps the corks from drying out. Cool, moist temperatures also help preserve root vegetables, potatoes, even apples.

■ Store related items together.
You don't want to stick the Christmas tree stand on one side of the room and the ornaments on the other behind a mountain of boxes.

■ Keep things accessible.
Arrange things so you can get at them easily. Don't pile boxes and containers so high or deep that you can't see behind them or have to pull stacks down to get at what's on the bottom.

■ Label containers
with BIG, **BOLD** lettering on the side, where it's visible. If you're feeling especially ambitious, list the contents on the side of the box, as well.

■ Don't be lazy.
When putting something back in storage, always return it to the same place you took it from.

Blowing Out the Cobwebs:

Spring Cleaning

For most guys, Spring Cleaning sounds like an old-fashioned ritual our grandmothers might have undertaken. But anyone, male or female, can feel the impulse to blow out

PRIORITY LEVEL:
Medium

NEEDS TO BE DONE:
Once a year
(but it's more
cleaning than
you've ever
done in your
life)

SPRING CLEANING

the cobwebs in the spring and shake off the winter doldrums. If you're a housekeeping Dad, you might consider channeling that impulse into cleaning.

For some of us, an annual Spring Cleaning is the only thing that keeps our houses from tipping over the edge into the garbage heap. For others, it's an opportunity to vacuum the refrigerator coils and starch those lace curtains. Whichever camp you fall into, start by doing all the tasks you'd do in a weekly clean—and you know what those are by now, right?— then take it to the next level. Be realistic about what you want to/ought to/must do and allot yourself a time limit for each task. I'll give you time guides for each job, but depending on how thorough or motivated you are, you could wrap it up in a day or take a week to do it.

This annual job is usually shared with a spouse, especially since it includes mutual household decisions, as well as agreements about what to throw out. How many of the recommended tasks in this chapter you actually do depends on what you and your wife feel is an acceptable level of clean. Whatever you decide, open your windows, get your supplies ready (see pages 8–9 for Dad's Own Tool Kit), and spring forward!

Ready, Set, Clean

Spring Cleaning means cleaning both the contents and their housing and then putting everything back in an organized way. Whatever you do, don't begin pulling things off the shelves until there's a plan. That means having a very good idea of exactly where and when they'll go back up. Here are some tips for successful deconstruction:

■ *Tackle one thing at a time.* That way, if you can't finish everything in one session, you'll still have livable space in your house.

■ *Protect your back.* When you lift something, keep your feet shoulder-width apart, bend your knees, tighten your abs, and lift with your leg muscles. Don't try to lift anything that is too heavy or is an awkward shape.

■ *Don't start cleaning until the cabinet or closet is completely empty.* Yeah,

I know, it's not the biggest deal if you miss a shelf, but if you've taken the trouble to go this far, why not do it right?

■ *See whether there's anything else you can throw away.* Chances are, you missed a bottle of expired Robitussin or can do without three of your ten flannel work shirts. Remember, one more item tossed means one less item to store.

■ Roll up your sleeves and really scrub, making sure to get into every nook and cranny. This is your one chance all year to eradicate dust, mold, mildew, cobwebs, and unidentifiable crud. Make it count.

Dad's Big-Time Assault on Clutter

When it comes to ridding your house of clutter, Spring Cleaning is the optimal dump time. After all, you can't even get to the actual *cleaning* until you *pick up and pare down.* But it all comes down to the same essentials:

ROOMS TO CONCENTRATE ON:
All

TIME:
1 to 2 hours per room

1. Recognize what clutter is. Clutter isn't just old junk, it's anything that's clogging up your house or your life, and that includes clothing, kitchen appliances, DVDs, and CDs, as well as old newspapers and magazines, expired foods, and canned or dried foods you never use. If you have no room to put the useable things away or store them, you have to start divesting.

2. Assign time limits. Give yourself a time goal and strive to meet it: "For one hour, I'll work on the closet in the hallway" or "For twenty minutes, I'll clear off my desk." Break the work down into small chunks and it becomes much more manageable.

3. Set must-act-now deadlines. Find reasons you have to get things done and then set a nonnegotiable due

SPRING CLEANING

date. If you need external motivation, do something like inviting your in-laws to come for your wife's birthday—you'll be forced to get the spare bedroom in shape before they arrive.

4. Let it go (or learn to be ruthless). Keeping heaps of stuff because "you might need it one day" ensures that you never will need it. For the vast majority of things, if you haven't worn it or used it for more than a year, let it go. (There'll always be the few sentimental exceptions like my old blue T-shirt from college. Either it stays or I go.)

5. Buckets, boxes, and bags. Before you begin, get a bunch of boxes for charitable donations and plenty of strong garbage bags for stuff going directly to the dump, then sort the castoffs accordingly.

Cleaning Your World: Ceilings and Walls

Before you start, clear away any cobwebs using the dusting attachment of your vacuum (see page 107) or sweep with a dry Swiffer or with a microfiber cloth wrapped around the head of your broom. Don't use a regular broom or you'll

ROOMS TO CONCENTRATE ON:
Kitchen and bathroom

TIME:
About 1 hour per room

Spot Cleaning

The stain-erasing sponge is good for general smears and streaks, including grubby fingerprints, on painted walls. If you have smudges or smears on wallpaper, try a muslin eraser bag, available at artist supply stores. It's a very gentle way to remove marks without streaking or removing color.

Unless your walls are particularly sooty or grimy, spot-cleaning is preferable to wet cleaning, especially if you have newer paint. As oil-based paints have become obsolete (and even illegal for indoor use in many states), it's increasingly likely that you have water-based latex paint on your wall. You can wash a semigloss or gloss latex without worrying, but don't use a lot of water on a flat-finish latex or you may find you're literally scrubbing the paint off the wall.

just release the particles onto everything below. Take up any rugs from the floor.

If you don't have an extender attachment, you'll need a ladder or steady chair for this job. Put a fresh head on your sponge mop. Fill a basin with warm water and all-purpose cleaning liquid. Mop the ceiling just as you'd mop the floor, with long strokes that overlap at the edges. Be sure to rinse your mop head after every few strokes so you don't leave dirty streaks behind.

The idea here is to start at the ceiling and work your way down, following the dripping grime with your sponge, rag, or mop. If you wash your walls before your ceiling, they will inevitably streak, which means doing them over. Isn't it already enough that you're doing them at all?

Once the ceiling's clean and drying, turn your attention to the walls. You can use either the mop, or a sponge or rag (if you choose either of the latter, you'll definitely need something sturdy to stand on). Start at the top and take the dirt down with you. Keep in mind that different wall surfaces need to be cleaned in different ways.

For painted walls, sprinkle either baking soda or an all-purpose cleanser on a warm, damp sponge or a clean, damp sponge mop. (If you'd prefer to use a rag, use white or off-white discarded T-shirts, as the

The Nitty Gritty: Room by Room

In Spring Cleaning, you put extra elbow grease into basic tasks and you expand their scope: Wash the floors . . . *and* the walls *and* the ceiling. It's only once a year. Here are some of the special efforts you should consider making in every room:

Kitchen

■ Suck out the dust and old food crumbs in your cabinets, drawers, and under the range hood, using the crevice tool on your vacuum cleaner.

■ Move the refrigerator and stove from the wall and clean behind and under them (see page 174). Vacuum the coils behind the refrigerator for more efficient running and to save on electricity.

■ Replace or wash the range's ventilation filter.

■ Defrost the freezer if necessary (most models of refrigerators are self-defrosting).

■ Clean and sterilize trash and garbage cans.

Bathroom

■ Examine caulk around toilet, sink, bathtub, and shower and make sure water is not leaking anywhere. If it is or if the caulk is dry and brittle, replace it.

■ Take down the showerhead and clean out all the lime scale and mineral deposits by soaking it in a bucket filled with 1 quart warm water and 1 cup white vinegar for at least 20 minutes. Wipe clean with a sponge or paper towel before replacing it. Use a damp sponge and a sprinkle of cleanser to scrub the tub and sink drain catchers.

■ Replace or launder the shower-curtain liner (see page 72)— something that should be done seasonally and not just in the spring. Take down and launder the fabric shower curtain.

■ Unload the shower caddy, remove it, and wash it (many can

SPRING CLEANING

even be tossed in the dishwasher); throw out products that are never used.

■ Wash and sanitize the toilet brush and holder—better still, replace them—as well as the clothes hamper.

■ Clean out and reorganize the medicine cabinet, vanity, and cupboards. Throw away anything that isn't used or has expired, especially medications (be sure your kids can't get to them). Wash shelves. If it's especially dingy or worn, replace contact paper on shelves.

■ Vacuum the fan covers plus vents or radiators using the dusting attachment of your vacuum cleaner.

Living Spaces

■ Dust all components of the TV and stereo systems—and don't forget the speakers.

■ Clean lamps and shades (see page 177).

■ Shake out small rugs and hang in the sun.

■ Beat the dust out of sofa cushions outdoors and give rugs and upholstery a deep cleaning (see page 175).

■ Send Oriental rugs to professionals.

■ Clean the fireplace (see sidebar).

DAD *to* DAD

Check your fireplace flue for soot buildup and have the chimney cleaned by a professional once a year if you use it regularly in winter. Vacuum the fireplace and clean the surrounding stone or bricks if necessary. There's a special chemical used for this purpose that's pretty toxic, so you may want to leave fireplace cleaning to the pros.

Bedrooms

■ Clean out jewelry boxes and valets and polish the jewelry.

■ Clean light fixtures and bookshelves (see pages 171 and 176).

■ Dust off and polish all shoes and organize them on shoe racks.

■ Toss lone socks, pit-stained T-shirts, holey underwear.

SPRING CLEANING

dye in colored fabrics could leak out onto the wall.)
Wipe quickly in a long up-and-down motion, focusing
on one area at a time. Be sure to overlap strokes so
you don't miss any spots, and rinse and squeeze out
your sponge or mop often. Wipe walls dry to prevent

SPRING CLEANING

streaking. Note that not all types of paint are washable (the gloss and semigloss typically used in kitchens and bathrooms are). If you're not sure, don't take the chance of washing off the paint. In this case, it may be easier to repaint—and definitely use a gloss or semigloss this time around!

Regular wallpaper is usually washable; just follow the directions for cleaning painted walls. Be sure you squeeze out your sponge or mop head often, as excess water may cause the wallpaper to peel. See a professional to get nonwashable wallpaper clean. Unusual and exotic wall coverings usually cannot be washed. For something like silk, don't even try to clean it yourself.

When you come upon splotches of who-knows-what sticking to your walls, especially common in the kitchen around the garbage, stove, and above the sink, moisten the spots and apply a cleanser or baking soda. Go do something else for about ten minutes. When you come back, you should be able to easily wipe off even the most hardened crud.

With kids come crayon marks, and if you have aspiring artists at your house, all walls—not just in the kitchen and their rooms, but everywhere—are probably their "gallery." So get out the super stain-erasing sponge (see Dad's Own Tool Kit, pages 8–9) and put it to work. If you don't have one, use a regular sponge. But before you do, heat the "exhibits" with a blow dryer to soften them (crayons are essentially wax, which means they melt). Then dab clean with a damp sponge and your chosen cleaning product.

DAD *to* DAD

Lighting fixtures in all rooms tend to become insect graveyards that we ignore when changing a bulb. So at least once a year, unscrew the glass or plastic cover, dump the carcasses, and wash it in the sink with mild dish soap and warm water. I've been known to put glass fixtures in the dishwasher, but be careful with plastic, as some isn't strong enough to withstand machine washing.

More Laundry Than One Man Should Be Allowed to Do

The change of seasons is a great time to launder those linens that lie on or around your bed, hang on your windows, and live anywhere else you have removable fabric prone to collecting dust, pet hair, and odors. Do it all in one day and get it over with. Make a pile for dry-clean only and sort the rest by color and fabric (see page 79) and head to the laundry room.

ROOMS TO CONCENTRATE ON: All, especially the bedroom

TIME: 1 1/2 hours per load (includes taking stuff down, washing, drying, and replacing)

■ Remove all bed linens, including dust ruffles and the mattress pad, and toss them in the washer. Let the mattress air out for a couple of hours, then give it a flip (see page 121).

■ Vacuum drapes and curtains in each room before removing them. Once they are down, you'll have easier access to wash your windows, so coordinate these two tasks. Decide which curtains can go in the washer and which should be dry-cleaned.

■ Take the quilt or bedcover to the dry cleaner to freshen it up.

■ Remove all slipcovers and launder according to the directions on the tag, or put them in the pile for the dry cleaner. Vacuum the furniture using the crevice tool, and get under the upholstery with the upholstery tool. If you're feeling especially ambitious, steam clean under upholstery, as well.

■ If your machine is large enough, you can wash a duvet yourself on a warm, gentle cycle. Tumble dry with a couple of tennis balls to puff up the down.

For Spring Cleaning, You *Do* Do Windows

Before you begin, vacuum the sills and around the frames; take down curtains and blinds for washing (see page 177).

ROOMS TO CONCENTRATE ON: All that have windows

TIME: 1 day (preferably not a rainy one)

Windows can be some of the filthiest surfaces in the home. Outside, dirt and pollution build up, blocking the view. Inside, grime culprits run the gamut from cooking grease to pets' pawprints and more. In addition to cleaning, each spring you may have to take down and store storm windows and wash and put up screens for warm weather.

Here are some tips for getting the job done quickly and well:

■ Work with a partner if possible. While you're wiping down the inside, ask someone to watch from the outside to make sure you hit every spot and don't streak. Whether with a partner or solo, wash the inside of windows from side to side and the outside from top to bottom so you can locate any streaking problems.

■ Try washing the inside of windows with a cloth soaked in white vinegar instead of glass cleaner. Or spray with a solution of 3 tablespoons ammonia, 1 tablespoon vinegar, and 3 cups water.

■ To get hard-water spots off your windowsills, use a soft rag soaked in rubbing alcohol diluted with warm water. Rub over the surface. The spots won't disappear altogether, but the sills will look freshly painted.

■ Use an old toothbrush or cotton swab to clean the inside corners of windows.

■ Vacuum window and door screens and wash using a brush and a mixture of warm water and a mild household soap or detergent. Use fast-drying model-airplane glue to patch small holes in screens.

SPRING CLEANING

New Frontiers in Vacuuming

For routine cleaning, we just run the Hoover over carpets and floors and call it a day, but for Spring Cleaning, a whole new frontier opens up:

■ *Under and behind the couch, bed, armoire, bookshelves.* You'd be amazed at what can get between furniture and a wall in a seemingly clean room. Dust bunnies nothing—dust stegosaurs is more apt.

■ *Under and behind the refrigerator and stove.* These appliances actually do pull out. You'll have a brand-new respect for Cheerios' uncanny ability to travel *everywhere.* Also lift your range hood and vacuum well under it. (Just be careful to unplug your electric or electric-start range first, and steer clear of any gas line.)

ROOMS TO CONCENTRATE ON: All

TIME: 1 hour per room (including moving and replacing furniture)

■ *Sofas, love seats, upholstered chairs.* Use the upholstery tool on your vacuum for surfaces and the crevice tool to get down into the cracks. Be sure you pay attention to what you're sucking up: Loose coins can wreck your vacuum.

■ *Moldings, baseboards, windowsills, heating vents, tops of tall furniture.* The best-loved homes of cobwebs everywhere. Connect the dusting brush attachment to your vacuum cleaner and suck away.

■ *Lampshades and blinds.* These can be vacuumed —carefully—using the dusting attachment. If lampshades are delicate, use a clean paintbrush instead.

■ *Drapes and curtains.* Lots of dust, as well as pet hair, tends to collect

DAD *to* **DAD**

Forget about those girly, sweet-smelling carpet deodorizers. Freshen carpets by sprinkling them with baking soda. Leave it on for about 30 minutes, then vacuum.

on these, so vacuum before washing or dry-cleaning or they might not come clean.

■ *Books*. Just like anything else, they get dusty. Before you spend time cleaning them, downsize the collection (see page 176). You can't "wash" books, but you can vacuum them. Just be careful: Keep the vacuum at a very low setting and use the dusting attachment. If some of your books are too fragile for this—dime-store paperbacks, not family-heirloom first editions—it might be time to let them go.

The Deep Clean

At least once a year, you want to give your carpets and upholstery a nice, wet cleaning by using a carpet steamer. (The exception is Oriental rugs, which need to be sent out for

ROOMS: **All that have rugs**

TIME: **1 hour per room**

professional cleaning.) You can buy steamers fairly cheaply these days, but because they take up so much storage room the rest of the year, consider renting instead. For best results when you steam clean your carpet and upholstery:

■ Move all the furniture out of the room. If this isn't possible, protect all furniture feet with aluminum foil. (You will still have to move the furniture around in the room so you can get every inch of carpet cleaned.)

■ Before you begin using the steamer, vacuum and then treat heavily soiled areas with prespray, following manufacturer's directions. Use special presprays to treat pet stains and odors if needed.

■ Prepare the steamer, following manufacturer's directions. In most machines, this means filling a reservoir with hot water and the recommended amount of carpet-cleaning solution.

■ Just like with vacuuming, start from the farthest corner and work your way to the entrance with overlapping strokes. The key is to go twice over each stroke: once with the spray button depressed, once without.

SPRING CLEANING

■ Using the upholstery attachment, you can clean furniture in the same way. Try not to oversaturate so you don't damage the frame or stuffing or the floor underneath.

■ It's ideal—though probably not possible— to wait overnight before walking on the carpet or using the furniture.

At least wait a couple of hours and speed-dry it by opening windows and turning on fans.

■ Keep your carpets cleaner longer by steaming over them again with a vinegar-water rinse made up of 1 cup white wine vinegar to 1 gallon water. Do this *after the carpet is dry.*

Hitting the Books

There's an old saying that getting rid of books cluttering your shelves helps make room for new ideas. Speaking to fellow book lovers who might be equally reluctant to prune, let me point out that it wasn't as bad as I thought:

■ Unless the book is of *actual* value and you're "collecting" it, let it go if you haven't opened it for the last ten years. Lose the college textbooks, novels that were dull the first time around, and gift books you've never cracked open.

■ Look up high for the things you'll probably never read again. Books you're not that interested in have a tendency to levitate to the higher shelves.

■ Cookbooks are not sacred. If you've never cooked out of it, or if you did and the dish was no good, let it go.

■ Technical books become dated very

quickly. If you're hanging on to your HTML manuals from ten years ago, say bye-bye. The Web and you have moved on.

■ Donate your books to charity (and take a tax write-off) or sell them to a used-book store.

■ When culling books, go with your gut. If you *really* want to keep it, do, or you'll lie awake nights thinking about it. If you feel this way about every book but desperately need the space, tell yourself, "I can only feel this way about 50 percent of my books. The rest have to go." (Their going as far as the garage might be a little secret between you and your books.)

The Old Brush-off: Doing Dusting Right

If you've been keeping up with weekly dusting, this chore will not be as taxing as it would be otherwise. Just note: The seasonal dusting chores should be done *before* the weekly ones or you'll have to redo the regular stuff.

Here are some extra places that need your attention at Spring Cleaning:

ROOMS TO CONCENTRATE ON: **All**

TIME: 1 hour per room (including clearing away and replacing items)

■ *Crown moldings as well as the tops of window and door frames.* You may not be able to see what's up there, but you can breathe it, which is reason enough to wipe them clean with a microfiber cloth or a damp sponge.

■ *Baseboards, ceiling vents, radiators, and heating ducts.* Vacuum these using the crevice attachment.

■ *Blinds.* They can be dusted with a soft, never-before-used paintbrush. If they're particularly dirty, take them down and soak them in warm water in the bathtub or take them outside and spray them with your garden hose. Be sure to clean both sides.

How to Clean a Lamp

Wash lamp shades made of stitched fabric or plastic in the bathtub with warm water and a few drops of dishwashing soap. After rinsing, wipe dry with a clean rag. For glued fabric shades, loosen dust with a microfiber cloth or feather duster, then gently clean with dry-cleaning fluid and a clean rag. To clean parchment shades, use only a dry duster. If that doesn't work, a very lightly dampened rag will do the trick—just be careful, as these shades are very delicate.

Please note: You should never submerge a lamp base in water. Simply spritz with an all-purpose cleaner and wipe clean with a paper towel.

SPRING CLEANING

■ *Picture frames.* Dust these with a microfiber cloth or feather duster and polish the glass with glass cleaner and a paper towel.

■ *Ceiling fans.* Remove the blades and clean them depending on the material: Wood blades can be washed with Murphy Oil Soap and polished with Pledge and a paper towel; plastic ones can be scrubbed with a sponge and an all-purpose cleaner (some can even be put in the dishwasher).

■ *Display items.* Don't bother dusting vases, crystal, and silver if you can help it. Most dishwashers have a fine china and crystal setting, so use it.

Yearly Tasks

The inside of your home is only part of the battle. Spring is a good time to clean the outside of your house. Rent a power washer to scrub down the front, sides, and back.

Here's a quick list of other things that should be checked at least once a year to make sure they're working properly. Then they should be cleaned, repaired, or replaced if needed.

- [ ] **all screens**
- [ ] **air-conditioning grills and filters (seasonally)**
- [ ] **circuit breakers (turn them all on and off)**
- [ ] **garage-door tracks**
- [ ] **sliding-door tracks**
- [ ] **porch and deck**
- [ ] **walkways and stairs**
- [ ] **air-conditioner compressor**
- [ ] **furnace filter**
- [ ] **roof (look for leaks)**
- [ ] **septic tank and surrounding area (for flooding or odor)**
- [ ] **vent duct of the dryer (also check the dryer exhaust a few times a year to ensure that there's no lint buildup)**
- [ ] **water heater (drain as necessary and check the relief valve)**
- [ ] **weatherstripping (apply in winter, remove in spring)**
- [ ] **basement sump pump, if you have one**

The 30-Minute Pre-In-law Assault on Dirt Program

You just found out your in-laws or your own spic-and-span parents are stopping by, and the house is a mess. You don't have time to read the whole book right now. So here's a plan that allows you to get the house looking good— or good enough—in just 30 minutes. On your mark, get set, go!

Start with the bathroom

5 MINUTES

■ Skip the all-clear—just throw away anything that doesn't belong (empty toothpaste box someone forgot to toss) and heave towels, washcloths, and bathmat into the hamper (or hallway if no hamper in bathroom).

■ Sprinkle cleanser into toilet bowl and let sit.

■ Spray all-purpose cleaner over toilet seat, tank top, and pedestal and wipe clean with a paper towel.

■ Quickly scrub bowl with toilet brush and flush.

■ Spray all-purpose cleanser on countertops and sink. There's no time to remove objects on counters, so just wipe *around* them, then wipe sink. Wipe mirror with paper towels and glass cleaner.

■ Unless the drop-ins are staying with you, you don't need to clean the shower or bathtub. Just pull the curtain closed. If they are staying, do it quickly— forget about soap scum, dull brass, drain, etc. Spray the shower or tub walls with all-purpose cleaner and sprinkle the tub with cleanser. Splash walls with water from shower; wipe tub with sponge and rinse clean.

■ Replace the towels with fresh ones.

Move to the kitchen

10 MINUTES

■ Throw away anything that doesn't belong (empty boxes, chip bags, soda bottles) and toss all dishtowels into doorway for pickup.

■ Get rid of dishes in sink and on countertops by putting them in dishwasher or washing them.

■ Wipe down all countertops and sink with all-purpose cleaner. (Wipe around items that stay out on the counter.)

■ Sweep floor debris into dustpan and empty it into trash, or shave off a few seconds by vacuuming if vac is handy.

■ Dampen sponge mop and apply cleanser or baking soda. Quickly swab high-traffic areas, waiting until you're through to rinse and squeeze out the mop.

■ Spritz handle of the refrigerator door and wipe clean. Repeat with any part of fridge door that shows (no need to clear off the artwork or photos), range top, dishwasher front, and switch plates.

■ Take out trash and replace liner.

■ Replace dirty dishtowels.

Move to the living room

5 MINUTES

■ Quickly stack all magazines and books into neat piles.

■ Pick up all stray socks, forgotten shoes, sweaters, etc., and hurl them at doorway. Loudly call kids: "Come and get your things or else I'll . . ."

■ Fluff up and straighten furniture cushions and any pillows; fold and stack blankets.

■ Slip loose DVDs and CDs into jewel cases and stack them on or beside entertainment unit.

■ Give all surfaces a once-over with a feather duster or microfiber cloth.

■ Vacuum high-traffic areas.

■ If kids haven't come for their stuff, put the whole pile anywhere you know Grandma and Grandpa won't be going.

Dash to the kids' rooms

(Grandma and Grandpa may want to play with the little ones in their room. Suggestion: Clean only one of the kids' rooms and try and contain the folks there.)

4.25 MINUTES

■ Make beds.

■ Throw all clothes from floor and furniture into hamper.

■ Toss shoes into closet.

■ Jam toys into nearest box or bin.

■ Put extra toys and stuffed animals under the bed.

■ Vacuum high-traffic areas.

Finish up with your own bedroom

(Only if there's time. If there isn't, just close the door. Your privacy will probably be respected.)

4.75 MINUTES

- Make bed.
- Throw all clothes from floor into hamper.
- Toss shoes into closet.
- Neatly stack magazines, newspapers, and other paper.
- Sweep jewelry and beauty products into top drawer of bureau or night table, as well as things you don't want your mother-in-law to see.
- Vacuum high-traffic areas.

Final sweep

1 MINUTE

- Pick up all the dirty laundry you've amassed in each room and take it to the washing machine.

APPENDIX

Appendix I

Dad's Guide to Getting Help

The first time I hired a house cleaner, two very professional women whipped my place into shape with a speed and efficiency that left me both stunned and humbled. They cleaned *everything* and did the laundry, too, all in less than three hours. You might want to consider hiring someone specifically to help with the tasks of Spring Cleaning.

There's no shame in getting help, even if you're a stay-at-home parent. If you have small kids or freelance work, or any other reason, having a regular house cleaner can be a real sanity saver. And don't just think about cash flow; consider what your time is worth. If the same amount of work would have taken you two whole days, then three or four hours' worth of professional cleaning can actually be a bargain.

How to Hire

Word of mouth is the best way to find a professional house cleaner, because you're more likely to find a person who's reliable and trustworthy—very important for someone who may end up with a set of your house keys. You could also look into using a cleaning service, which may be more expensive but will screen anyone who comes into your home, as well as provide services an individual might not, like cleaning beneath and behind the stove or refrigerator.

APPENDIX

Here are some things to ask a potential cleaner:

■ *Will you bring your own cleaning supplies or do I provide them?* This can make a significant difference in the overall cost.

■ *If I'm supplying cleaning products, what exactly do you need?*

■ *What are your standard tasks?* Most cleaners have a set list of what they do, and it can vary a lot.

■ *Who* exactly *will be coming?* Services send varying teams of cleaners, but an individual cleaner should come him- or herself or let you know well in advance if someone will be filling in.

■ *How flexible are you about extra tasks?* You may want your cleaner to wipe down the baseboards in your kitchen or pull the sofa away from the wall and vacuum underneath. If specific tasks are important to you, ask before engaging someone long-term.

Chores to Expect from a Pro

What to expect:

■ Light dishwashing

■ Laundry, if agreed upon at hiring or requested at specific visits, sometimes for an additional fee

■ Changing bed sheets

■ Sweeping, mopping, vacuuming all the floors

■ Wiping down all kitchen surfaces, such as counters and stove

■ Complete bathroom cleaning, from floors to fixtures

■ Wiping down or polishing furniture and surfaces

■ Polishing mirrors

■ General tidying and surface clearing (within reason)

What not to expect *(unless you pay extra):*

■ Oven cleaning

■ Washing windows, walls, or ceilings

■ Polishing silver

■ Cleaning out the fridge

■ Laundry (this one varies; some do it as a basic task, others charge an extra fee or refuse to do it at all)

■ Attic, basement, or garage cleaning

■ Cleaning (other than vacuuming) or beating rugs or carpets

■ Cleaning up excessive clutter

■ Disposing of garbage from waste baskets

Appendix II

Behind Closed Drawers

Going the Extra Mile in Kitchen Reorganization

The kitchen counters are no longer cramped and cluttered if you've followed the advice in the first chapter. But chaos may still lurk behind your cabinet doors and deep in the back of your kitchen drawers. Wouldn't it be great to prepare a complete meal from start to finish and never once have to stop and yell out: "Honey, where's the . . . ?" Even the most disheveled Dad can master having organized, functional kitchen cabinets and drawers—which means knowing where everything is and being able to get out what you need when you need it. This is a one-time job for a rainy day; but once you have these spaces organized, you'll be glad you did it.

Take one cabinet or drawer at a time and empty the contents onto your newly clean countertop. Now sort ruthlessly, paying special attention to doubles, extras, and detritus. Do you have a lot of "freebies" hanging around in there? How about crumpled, grease-stained takeout menus? When's the last time you used that kidney-shape salad bowl? And how many can openers does one family need?

Just like with your countertops, take a few minutes to think things through. You'll want to call your wife in to help strategize where everything should go.

Two heads are better than one, and both of you want to be familiar and comfortable with the new layout.

Your best plan of attack: Categorize. Devise a group concept for each available cabinet and drawer. Because you'll be working with a lot of small items, get some boxes to help sort things and label them with your cabinet categories. Also get extra boxes for stuff that's going to charity or out in the trash.

Here are a few specific things to keep in mind when putting everything back.

Food Storage

Store food in your upper cabinets so that everything you need to throw a meal together is at about eye level. Sort dry goods according to type: all the pasta here, all the canned goods there, and so forth. Toss out-of-date, unidentifiable, or never-to-be-used food.

If you're overburdened with, say, canned tomatoes or soup, start using them up and quit buying them until you actually run out. If you've got a stack of something you rarely use, say ten cans of fruit cocktail, put it in a box labeled "Local Food Bank" or "Kids' Food Drive"—and make sure it gets there.

When reloading food into your cabinet, think about what you use the least and put those items high up and/or in the rear. Save the front of the shelves that are easiest to reach for what you use most often. If you have two of something, store one behind the other. If you have more than two, take the extras and store them in another cabinet or the basement, or put them

Those Who Live in Glass Houses . . .

Admit it: Don't you use the same coffee cup every morning?

Yet it's common for two parents and two kids to have about 16 cups clogging the shelves—the standard cups and mugs, the ones with cutesy sayings, and the giveaway promotional mugs—and only drink from the front three or four. And then there are glasses. . . . Take a hard look at your drinkware and begin to pare. Ruthlessly. Recycle what you can, discard the crummy stuff, and give the rest away to a local charity.

in one of the charity boxes. Put cans on lower shelves; boxes and bags on higher ones. (It's much less painful to have a box of dry macaroni fall on your head than a can of tomatoes.) Finally, don't overstock your cabinets—relying on the cabinet door as the "fourth wall" just sets booby traps that your unsuspecting wife or 12-year-old will undoubtedly trip.

Dish, Plate, and Bowl Storage

How high are your dishes stacked? We used to keep our small plates on top of the large dinner plates, and the salad bowls on top of those. Anytime I needed a dish, I had to lift 15 others out of the way.

Ever since my wife and I were able to compromise and no longer have everything we have ever owned cramming up the works in our cabinets, our lives have become much easier. By getting rid of a dozen stained plastic storage tubs, I was able to fit three separate stacks of the main eating dishes: large plates, smaller plates, and bowls. Now I just open the cabinet, take out what I need, and close the cabinet.

So here's what you do: Stack all your dishware on the kitchen table. Think through your day, your week, and make it a point to replace *only* what you *actually* use—and to leave enough space to reach what you need at any particular time without shifting or lifting what you don't need. You'll have to do some dickering with your wife about what stays and what goes, but she might let you store that ornate stoneware serving pot in the basement if you toss out those gas-station-giveaway glasses you've had since college.

That Unexplored Realm Under the Sink

This is where the heavy-duty cleaners and cleaning tools, like sponges, spare mop heads, scrub brushes, rubber gloves, and more are generally kept. But it's apt to become the black hole of Calcutta unless you impose some order on it. So first pare down your supplies to only what you use, then organize them in even the most elementary way: glass cleaners in one group, wood cleaner and polish in another, and so on. Buy a few storage caddies—or recycle those cool

APPENDIX

Free the Freebies

Do you collect them in a drawer? Toss them behind the cereal? You know what I mean: those little packets of soy sauce, ketchup, mustard, and salt plus straws, plastic utensils, and whatnot that came free with your takeout and you were too cheap to throw them out. Set your freebies free—and free up the drawer space. (Okay, if you must, keep a couple of each in the unlikely event that you have a duck sauce crisis.)

wooden boxes that hold clementines. If you have small children, be sure to install a lock on this cabinet.

You might store garbage bags you save from the store here, but don't just toss them in and slam the door—they take up a ridiculous amount of space that way. Either get one of those bag-holding gadgets that mounts on the back of the door, try one of the cloth tube-shape bag holders, or flatten down smaller bags inside a larger one.

So Many Gadgets, So Little Space!

Most utensil drawers are a mishmash of items we've unthinkingly collected over the years, so shove aside the corn butterers, fish forks, and swizzle sticks and take a good look at your basic equipment: Really, how many vegetable peelers does one cook need? Here's a quick list, by category, of things you may want to keep in those drawers.

Top drawer closest to your work space

This is where you want to keep those utensils and gadgets you use regularly for cooking:

- spatulas (1 plastic for nonstick pans and 1 metal)
- fruit/vegetable peeler
- measuring spoons
- wooden spoons (2 for cooking and 1 for baking)
- slotted spoon
- meat mallet
- potato masher
- garlic press
- heatproof rubber spatula
- whisk

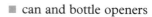
- Microplane (a worthwhile luxury)
- poultry shears

- can and bottle openers
- corkscrew

Alternatively you can store frequently-used kitchen utensils in a ceramic pot near your work space. It's often easier to find what you need than rummaging around in the catchall utility drawer.

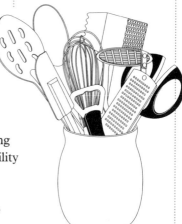

Top drawer, more remote

This is where your daily-use forks, knives, and spoons go—you don't need to grab them as swiftly as the utensils used for cooking. The problem with this drawer is that it can quickly become a disaster when utensils slide out of their designated slots in the organizer because there are too many to fit in there. Remember: The more you have, the more you'll use, and the more you'll have to clean. Here's a simple equation for keeping on hand only what you need:

Number of family members + 3 (for guests and mealtime droppage) = number of forks, knives, and spoons you need to keep in this drawer. Take whatever is left over and store it in a box marked "for company" anywhere you have the space.

Middle drawer

Great for storing stuff you use once or twice during the day, such as aluminum foil, plastic wrap, sandwich bags, and paper napkins.

Bottom drawer

These are sometimes the deepest of the drawers, so you want to maximize space. Do your plastic storage tubs stack neatly? Why not stash them here instead of taking up an entire cabinet to store them?

INDEX

Index

INDEX

INDEX